D0943877

The
Elements
of
Mentoring

The
Elements
of
Mentoring

75 Practices of Master Mentors

3RD EDITION

. . .

W. Brad Johnson *and*
Charles R. Ridley

St. Martin's Press ❧ New York

THE ELEMENTS OF MENTORING. Copyright © 2018, 2008, 2004 by W. Brad Johnson and Charles R. Ridley. All rights reserved. Printed in the United States of America. For information, address St. Martin's Press, 175 Fifth Avenue, New York, NY 10010.

www.stmartins.com

Library of Congress Cataloging-in-Publication Data

Names: Johnson, W. Brad, author. | Ridley, Charles R., author.
Title: The elements of mentoring : 75 practices of master mentors / W. Brad Johnson and Charles R. Ridley.
Description: 3rd edition. | New York : St. Martin's Press, 2018. | Includes bibliographical references and index.
Identifiers: LCCN 2018001893| ISBN 9781250181268 (hardcover) | ISBN 9780230616837 (ebook)
Subjects: LCSH: Mentoring in business. | Mentoring in the professions. | Mentoring in education. | Employees—Counseling of. | Mentoring.
Classification: LCC HF5385 .J64 2018 | DDC 658.3/124—dc23
LC record available at https://lccn.loc.gov/2018001893

Our books may be purchased in bulk for promotional, educational, or business use. Please contact your local bookseller or the Macmillan Corporate and Premium Sales Department at 1-800-221-7945, extension 5442, or by email at MacmillanSpecialMarkets@macmillan.com.

Third Edition: June 2018

10 9 8 7 6 5 4 3 2 1

Contents

Arranging the Mentoring Relationship:

Celebrating Diversity: MATTERS OF HUMAN

Knowing Thyself as a Mentor: MATTERS OF INTEGRITY

When Things Go Wrong: MATTERS OF RESTORATION

Welcoming Change and Saying Goodbye: MATTERS OF CLOSURE

With love, gratitude, and endless admiration,
we dedicate this book to our children—our greatest mentees—
Jacob, Daniel, and Stanton; and Charles and Mary

Acknowledgments

We thank Laura Apperson, our acquisitions editor at St. Martin's Press for finding promise in our idea and delivering encouragement at all the right times.

I thank my wife, Laura Johnson, for her patience, love, and more patience. She brings grace, elegance, and endless kindness to a home full of guys. I am particularly indebted to my graduate school mentor, Charles R. Ridley, who embodies the elements of mentoring. His example piqued my ongoing interest in the power of good mentoring.

—W. B. J.

I thank my wife, Mary Ridley, who brings me immeasurable joy, embodies inner and outer beauty, and helps make our home a sanctuary. I am grateful to our children, who make us proud parents. A special acknowledgment goes to the many graduate students in psychology whom I have been privileged to mentor over the years. Without them, I would not have learned the crucial elements of mentoring. I especially am indebted to W. Brad Johnson. He is an exemplar of a mentee who has become a competent mentor in his own right.

—C. R. R.

Preface

The reasonable thing is to learn from those who can teach.
—SOPHOCLES

This is a short book, but not because there is little to say. Much has been written about the art and science of mentoring. In the last several years alone, more than a thousand books and journal articles have addressed the topic. There are research reports, narrative accounts, and manuals for professionals, spiritual leaders, and educators. In this book, we zero in on the basics and eliminate unnecessary words; our goal is to untangle the morass of research and writing on the topic. We offer readers a clear summary of the fundamental principles of mentoring—principles we deem to be universal. We do this without fluff, hype, and myth. These are simply the nuts and bolts of being a good mentor—nothing more.

Our heroes in the world of pithy writing are William Strunk and E. B. White. In their now-classic *The Elements of Style*, Strunk and White offer crucial rules for avoiding basic mistakes in composition. Rule 17, "Omit Needless Words," states: "Vigorous writing is concise. A sentence should contain no unnecessary words, a paragraph no unnecessary sentences, for the same reason that a drawing should have no unnecessary lines and a machine no unnecessary parts" (Strunk & White 2000, p. 23). In our view, a book on the crucial elements of mentoring also should contain nothing unnecessary. Our singular purpose is to distill the research-supported fundamentals on being an effective mentor.

In preparation for the writing of this book, we conducted an extensive search of the scholarly literature on mentoring and read nearly two thousand publications from business, psychology, education, and other fields. We gave more weight to research studies and downplayed "feel-good" pieces on the topic. We searched for findings with direct relevance to mentors; we combed the research for data-supported truths about what makes a mentor excellent. In *The Elements of Mentoring*, we funnel the voluminous mentoring literature into a concise guide for the practicing mentor. The result is a short list of the essential ingredients of mentoring: what new mentors need to know and what seasoned mentors will do well to remember. These are the "rules of engagement" for master mentors. A *master mentor* is someone who judiciously integrates clear communication, knowledge of human development, technical mentoring skills, emotional intelligence, ethical values, and honest personal reflection in daily mentoring practice for the benefit of individual mentees.

We introduce each element with an applied case study of excellent mentoring in practice. Each case study represents an amalgam of several good mentorships we have witnessed over the years. Although each case alone is fictitious, each offers a clear, real-world example of the best mentoring practice. We conclude each element with a terse summary of its basic ingredients—the *key components*. In the trenches, readers may quickly refer back to these salient summaries of each crucial mentoring element. The elements of mentoring cut across all academic disciplines, professions, and contexts. They hold true for managers, professors, leaders, clinical supervisors, and anyone else committed to mentoring.

These truths should be as compelling for teachers as for CEOs of multinational corporations.

Our own interest in mentoring stems from our extensive work with students, consulting clients, and research participants. We are psychologists and college professors with a background of researching and writing about mentorships. Brad Johnson is a clinical psychologist and a faculty member in both the Department of Leadership, Ethics, and Law at the U.S. Naval Academy and at the Graduate School of Education at Johns Hopkins University. Charles Ridley is a professor of counseling psychology at Texas A&M University. He is also an organizational consultant. Both of us have written extensively and have mentored scores of excellent graduate students. We are also a mentoring pair. Our own successful mentorship during Brad Johnson's graduate school career triggered an ongoing interest in the various facets of mentoring—particularly the elements of mentor excellence.

We have distilled the vast mentoring literature into 75 key elements for effective mentoring. When practiced in concert, they define the attitudes, values, and skills of the *master mentor*. The elements are clustered around seven primary themes—what excellent mentors do (matters of skill); the traits of excellent mentors (matters of style and presence); arranging the mentor–mentee relationship (matters of beginning); celebrating diversity (matters of human differences); knowing thyself as mentor (matters of integrity); when things go wrong (matters of restoration); and welcoming change and saying goodbye (matters of closure). An appendix provides a *Mentoring Code of Ethics* for quick reference when faced with an ethical tension, quandary, or conflict in a mentoring relationship. We conclude with a list of important references. These sources are for professionals or scholars who wish to read the research and scholarly literature in greater detail.

Mentoring relationships (mentorships) are dynamic, reciprocal, personal relationships in which a more experienced person (mentor) acts as a guide, role model, teacher, and sponsor of a less experienced person (mentee). Mentors provide mentees with knowledge, advice, counsel, support, and opportunity in the mentee's pursuit of full membership in a particular profession. Outstanding mentors are intentional about the mentor role. They select mentees thoughtfully, invest significant time and energy in getting to know their mentees, and deliberately offer the career and support functions most useful for their mentees. Mentoring is an act of generativity—a process of bringing into existence and passing on a professional legacy. In Homer's epic poem *The Odyssey*, Mentor was an Ithacan noble and trusted friend of Odysseus. He was charged with caring for Odysseus's son Telemachus when Odysseus departed for the Trojan War. Later in the poem, the goddess Athena assumes Mentor's form to guide, protect, and teach Telemachus during his travels. In this role, Mentor (and Athena) serves as coach, teacher, guardian, protector, and kindly guide. As a clarification, we prefer the term *mentee* when referring to the junior member of a mentorship. Although the word *protégé*—Latin for "to protect"—is still used sometimes by other authors, it conjures formal apprenticeship, hierarchy, and a sense of dependency on the part of the junior member.

Mentoring is more than a fad. It is a well-researched helping relationship. Mentoring is associated with positive personal and career outcomes. What are the outcomes of mentoring? First, research consistently demonstrates the following benefits for mentored persons: enhanced promotion rates, higher salaries, accelerated career mobility, improved professional identity, greater professional competence, increased career satisfaction, greater acceptance within the organization or profession, and decreased job stress and role conflict. Mentored individuals also are more likely to mentor others. Second, mentors themselves benefit through internal satisfaction and fulfillment, enhanced creativity and professional synergy, career and personal rejuvenation, development of a loyal support base, recognition by the organization for developing talent, and generativity (pleasure associated with shaping future generations). Organizational leaders increasingly appreciate the critical contribution of deliberate mentorship for succession planning, grooming the next generation of institutional leaders. Finally, organizations reap tangible benefits. When a culture of mentorship takes root in an organization, leaders often are pleased to notice increased productivity, enhanced organizational commitment, decreased turnover, and accelerated development of in-house talent. And mentored employees are more likely to remain committed to the organization. It is apparent that competent mentoring has the potential for win-win outcomes for mentees, mentors, and the organizations they serve.

Nearly any developmental career relationship—whether formally assigned or organically evolving—can take on the qualities of mentorship. In fact, we find it most helpful to frame mentoring as a relationship *quality* or *character*, not necessarily a distinct relationship category. Any advising, supervising, managing, leadership, or sponsoring relationship can take on the quality of mentorship as the mentor begins to offer more of the elements contained in this book and as the relationship becomes more supportive, trusting, reciprocal, and inspiring over time.

Whether you are a new supervisor or a seasoned mentor, we hope *The Elements of Mentoring* serves as an invaluable tool for developing and promoting junior talent. Earnest consideration and frequent practice of these elements is a first step on the road to becoming a master mentor. Our hope is that this tool will help to sharpen your edge, increase your self-confidence, and add an irreplaceable dimension of fulfillment and satisfaction to your life and career. We also hope you will share it with others.

W. BRAD JOHNSON
Annapolis, Maryland

CHARLES R. RIDLEY
College Station, Texas

The
Elements
of
Mentoring

What Excellent Mentors Do

MATTERS OF SKILL

So what is a mentor supposed to *do* anyway? If this question has crossed your mind, you are not alone. Although many of us have benefited from the teaching, coaching, and care of one or more mentors, some of us have never been mentored and might wonder how such a relationship actually should be structured. We wonder what to do once a decision to mentor is made. In this section of *The Elements*, our focus is on the tangible behaviors or functions of mentoring. Each of these functional mentoring elements requires a combination of knowledge, attitudes, and skills. Knowledge is informed understanding. You should understand how each distinct mentoring element is crucial for your mentee's development and how you might most effectively deliver it in your unique context or professional field. Attitude is a mentor's perspective or point of view. Each mentoring component will be useful only if it is approached in the right spirit and primarily for the benefit of the mentee. Ultimately, a mentor's knowledge and attitudes translate into a set of functional skills. Skill is behavior designed to serve a specific purpose. Many of the elements we discuss require experience and seasoning and mastering those results from deliberate practice. Only then will they be honed and sharpened.

The skills of mentoring are intended primarily to facilitate a mentee's career development. At various times throughout a mentee's career, a mentor sponsors a mentee for a new position, coaches a mentee through the nuances of a new task, introduces a mentee to key colleagues, or gives a challenging assignment intended to stretch a mentee beyond his or her comfort zone. Here the mentor is demonstrating *career functions*. At other times, the mentor directs attention to the mentee's emotional and personal development. A mentor may give much-needed affirmation, encourage the pursuit of dreams, lend emotional support, or engage in increasing collegial friendship with the mentee. Here the mentor is demonstrating *psychosocial functions*.

Each of the 24 elements included in this section are matters of skill. Each can be learned. With the appropriate attitudes (a sincere and generative interest in the growth of others—what we refer to as the character virtue of care) and necessary knowledge (something we hope *The Elements* helps you to achieve), we believe you have the prerequisites for mastering these mentoring functions. We ask you to keep in mind that these elements of mentoring are much like tools in the toolbox of a master mechanic. Discretion is needed for the appropriate use of the tools. Skillful mechanics know that they cannot use all of their tools at one time, that some tools may be inappropriate for certain jobs, and that some tools are more important than others. In a similar manner, mentors assess individual mentees to determine which combination of elements is most likely to be helpful at each stage in a mentee's development. We do not believe that this type of assessment can be achieved by using a rigid formula. Assessing mentees is really more a matter of growing wisdom and competence in the mentor role—a sort of *knowing* born of first-hand experience. Nevertheless, in the chapters that follow, mentors may find some of these elements particularly helpful: "Know Your Mentees," "Capitalize on Teachable Moments," "Listen

Actively," "Schedule Periodic Reviews or Evaluations," "Check Yourself for Unintentional Bias," and "Slow Down the Process." Overall, mentors need more than to simply have the right tools in their toolboxes. They need to know how to apply these tools selectively and thoughtfully to get good results. Such mentor wisdom is a product of steadily accruing experience, commitment, and humility. Chances are you will never be a perfect mentor.

I

Select Your Mentees Thoughtfully

As a successful senior manager in a thriving electronics company, Steve frequently supervised and interacted with junior managers and managerial trainees. Although he was courteous, fair, and helpful in these relationships, Steve was thoughtful when it came to committing time and resources to more in-depth mentorships. During a five-year period, he intentionally mentored four new managers—all of whom demonstrated strong potential and shared his interests in and commitment to the organization. Intentional mentoring requires deliberate and thoughtful planning. Steve was careful to consider a mentee's specific mentoring needs. Each of these mentees caught Steve's attention through his or her stellar job performance, initiative, and frequent interaction. Although he had the reputation of being an excellent mentor and although he was often approached by junior managers for career guidance, Steve was acutely conscious of his limited resources (e.g., time, energy, and opportunities for including mentees in his work). For this reason, he carefully scrutinized promising new managers, determined the level of chemistry or "match" in their interactions, and then firmly committed himself only to the number he believed he could carefully and successfully assist through the early phase of their careers.

Choosing mentees is similar to investing. You have limited resources, and you hope for good returns. Among the best returns on a mentoring investment are these: mentees who thrive in their careers and make outstanding contributions; organizations that enjoy high retention, commitment, and loyalty from employees; and mentors who savor the synergy of working with talented junior professionals who become the next generation of stars and leaders. To get these returns, mentors must behave like prudent investors. They start by carefully selecting their mentees. Mentors must have acumen to discern the type of traits, talents, and interests of their junior professionals that serve as a good match for a mentorship. Like any investment, the expectation is the payment of dividends for the mentor, mentee, sponsoring organization, or profession.

Selectivity matters for another reason. You cannot mentor everyone. No matter how energized, idealistic, and gifted you are, everyone has limitations. This means that taking on too many mentees is a sure way to compromise your own health, the quality of your mentoring, and your own performance at work. Excellent mentors appreciate the costs of mentoring. It takes time, emotional energy, and professional resources. Unless they are careful, competent mentors can fall into a trap.

What happens when a mentor fails at the task of selectivity? In attempting to mentor too many people or mentees with whom they are poorly matched, mentors dilute the power of mentoring in the lives of mentees. They also diminish their own enjoyment of the mentoring experience, which ironically is considered one of the greatest benefits of being a mentor. Well-intended but overextended mentors can pay a heavy price—sometimes to the point of becoming exhausted, detached, emotionally muted, or even cynical toward their mentees. Excellent mentors know when to say no. When they reach their threshold, they gracefully decline accepting new mentoring relationships, especially with poorly matched juniors. This protects their current cadre of mentees from lackluster mentoring, and it helps to ensure ample reserves of energy and focus for their mentoring efforts.

Look at the other side. What about the psychology of mentors who just can't say no? The obvious consequences are a failure to set limits, inadequate self-care, and, ultimately, burnout. They are perpetually overextended, hurried, and needlessly pressured, as anyone would attest. But the causes are less apparent than the consequences. Failure to set limits may indicate poor assertiveness skills or fear of rejection. It might represent an unhealthy need for approval or an insatiable need to be valued and appreciated. Being pursued by potential mentees might feed a mentor's need for importance or status. And failure to set limits could reflect a mentor's misunderstanding of the actual professional requirements and emotional demands of good mentorship. Whatever the cause, under these conditions, mentorships are likely to be marginalized.

What guidelines should mentors follow in initiating developmental relationships with prospective mentees? Research indicates that mentors in most fields generally select mentees with obvious talent and career potential. Juniors who earn the label "fast-tracker" based on their past achievements and the perception that they will be successful are usually appealing to mentors. These mentees favorably reflect the mentor's competence in developing talent, and they eventually may become valued colleagues to the mentor. Yet good mentorships can—and should— also be established with individuals who have not been labeled as "fast-trackers." Communication skills, emotional stability, ambition, initiative, intelligence, and loyalty are important traits that can supersede a label. In addition, mentors can be well served by seeking mentees who share their interests. Last, excellent mentors are conscious about seeking cultural and gender diversity among those they mentor.

In business settings, mentorships that begin informally often are more effective than those that are brokered or "arranged." The mutual understanding, respect, and trust that naturally evolve in an informally developed mentorship increase the chances that both parties will find the experience satisfying. We should always remember that mentorships, first and foremost, are relationships. As in a marriage, the freedom to choose for both the mentor and mentee provides grounding for mutual commitment and satisfaction. It's crucial that mentors be thoughtful and intentional when selecting their mentees.

KEY COMPONENTS

- *Honestly consider the maximum number of mentees you can mentor while ensuring excellence in the mentor role.*
- *Identify the personal qualities, interests, and aspirations of mentees that make them a good "match" before committing to a mentorship.*
- *Commit to mentor only after some period of informal work and interaction with a prospective mentee.*
- *Remain vigilant to symptoms of mentor burnout.*
- *Honestly consider your motivation for mentoring.*
- *Whenever possible, select a diverse portfolio of mentees.*

2

Be There

What Phil lacked in outgoing personality he more than made up for in calm, steady consistency. He was not Mr. Charisma, but he was present and dependable. As resident director for a large college dormitory, he was a supervisor and frequent mentor to numerous resident advisors—typically upper-class undergraduates designated as counselors and overseers of freshmen and sophomore dorm residents. Although Phil's plate was often full, he made it a priority to frequently engage his new advisors in the form of check-in phone calls, office drop-ins, and invitations to coffee or hot chocolate in the first-floor café. Even when he was attending graduate classes or away from campus, he made sure his advisors could contact him, and when they did, he was steady, reassuring, and encouraging. Whenever a student incident occurred, Phil always seemed to be nearby and prepared to offer the advisor backup and support. Moreover, Phil's door was always open—both figuratively and literally—and he was a willing coach and advocate for many of the advisors who, like Phil, were considering careers in human services or academic leadership. Phil's proactive contact with subordinates, his transparent commitment to their success, and his steady availability won him deep loyalty among the resident advisors and launched a significant number of rewarding mentorships.

In the early 1970s, the Jackson 5's "I'll Be There" became a hit song. Even today, people are moved by the touching lyrics, which speak of one person's availability and presence for another. Being there for another person speaks volumes, more than words or any other action could possibly convey.

Ask young people who they are likely to marry one day, and you'll probably get a range of romantic responses such as "the one person on earth who was created just for me." But the scientific evidence offers a more seemingly mundane snapshot of how we select life partners: we love the ones we're with. That is, most of us will probably marry someone we have worked with, studied with, gone to church with, or otherwise often encountered. Social psychologists refer to the connection between simple proximity and attraction as the *mere exposure effect* (Bornstein, 1989). In a nutshell, human beings become emotionally bonded to those people they frequently encounter and get to know.

The mere exposure effect works much the same way in mentorship. Effective mentors are accessible and approachable. They make time for mentees, ensuring more frequent interactions and more opportunity for engagement. Wise mentors recognize that simply being there is often the key to creating an effective mentor–mentee bond. To that end, mentors seek out and "check in" with mentees, especially those who are reluctant by temperament or circumstance to approach the mentor. They manifest an attitude of invitation and interest that tends to encourage mentee engagement, and, when possible, they stop what they are doing to greet a mentee and address a question or concern.

Being there broadcasts respect for the mentee and commitment to the mentee's development. Being there increases the frequency of interaction, thereby deepening a mentor's understanding of the mentee's strengths, relative limitations, and career dreams. Being there also communicates something powerful about the mentor's priorities; making regular time available to a mentee suggests that the mentor sees the mentee as valuable and time with the mentee as worthwhile. Mentors should not underestimate the power of these communications. Finally, being there allows the mentor to model professionalism and then to impart wisdom in the course of day-to-day exchanges.

So what's the introverted mentor to do? If you happen to be an introvert, chances are you don't arrive at work each morning savoring the prospect of engaging in long conversations or having frequent interactions with others. Take heart! Many outstanding mentors are introverted. But the introvert must be more deliberate and careful about initiating interactions with mentees. Remember, many talented junior professionals are reluctant to "bother" an accomplished and busy mentor. So, schedule routine meetings and remind yourself to seek out interactions with mentees.

Availability, more than any other factor, also predicts whether formal organizational mentoring programs—those in which the organization assigns mentor and mentee—will be successful. Research on assigned relationships indicates that frequency of interaction is one of the best predictors of whether a mentorship will find purchase, gain traction, and blossom into something genuinely meaningful to both parties. Apparently, the "magic" of mentoring hinges mostly on exposure and frequency of interaction.

KEY COMPONENTS

- *Be accessible to mentees.*
- *Make time and interaction with mentees a priority.*
- *Counter your own introversion by scheduling routine interactions with mentees.*
- *Refuse to allow other commitments to intrude on designated mentoring time.*

3
Know Your Mentees

Mary, a senior partner in a multinational law firm, noticed the exceptional work and unusual talent of Brian, a junior lawyer in her division. Mary then decided to mentor Brian. In the early phase of the mentorship, she watched Brian in various contexts and went out of her way to talk to him about his short-term plans, personal interests, and his career aspirations. She made arrangements to work with Brian on cases and gave him a variety of assignments in order for him to get a well-rounded applied education as a lawyer. Mary discerned Brian's strengths in the area of litigation and assigned him cases in this specialty. She also became proficient at "reading" Brian's nonverbal behavior, particularly his signals of distress. She responded to these indicators with inquiry and wise counsel—helping Brian to take stock of himself before working his way into a self-destructive frenzy.

Outstanding mentors study their mentees just as hard as they would study anything they want to understand deeply. They learn each mentee's distinct mix of talents and vulnerabilities. They observe mentees in various situations to ascertain their reactions based on the circumstances. They listen to them and show interest in their heartfelt dreams and aspirations. They are especially attentive to the mentee's fears and personal challenges—acknowledging them as real but refusing to allow the mentee to see obstacles as insurmountable.

What is the most important outcome of the deliberate study of a mentee? We propose that it is the ability to name the mentee's prominent gifts—naming them accurately, thoroughly, and always specific to the individual. Although each person you mentor will have a unique blend of talents and perhaps one or more area of notable capability, some mentees are not as certain about their gifts as you might initially think. Mentees often err in underestimating their abilities. Even the most gifted and promising students and junior professionals can suffer from the dreaded *imposter syndrome*. Most of us have been there at one time or another; we suffer those anxiety-inducing thoughts about our incompetence and lack of qualification and wonder if we got admitted or hired by mistake. In quiet agony, we wait to be outed as frauds and shown to the exit, although we secretly hope that no one finds us out. Excellent mentors are attuned to imposter worries and quick to counter them with copious doses of affirmation and encouragement.

In naming mentees' gifts and talents—making explicit what is often implicit—a powerful but necessary shift occurs in mentees' self-concepts. The shift sets the course for a more promising career. But the neophytes need the seasoned mentor's validation before the course is set into motion. Once mentees see themselves for who they really are, they can build on their strengths and overcome their weaknesses. These are the results of seeing themselves through the sharp lens of their mentor.

To obtain an insightful understanding of mentees, mentors need to have a personal relationship with them. And the type of understanding of which we speak is more than knowing a mentee's name, rank, and serial number. It is a knowledge garnered through substantial observation, frequent interaction, and intense involvement—a real relationship. Research shows that the frequency and quality of face-to-face interaction predict mentorship success. This means not only that excellent mentors are accessible and available but that they also demonstrate the skills of listening, caring, communicating openly, and giving constructive feedback. To conclude, taking the time to truly know mentees is arguably the most important of the mentoring functions.

KEY COMPONENTS
- *Deliberately study and learn about your mentees.*
- *Identify and label mentees' talents and strengths and then communicate these insights to them.*
- *Acknowledge mentee fears and comparative weaknesses without allowing them to distract or overwhelm.*
- *Look for patterns in mentees that occur across various settings, relationships, and types of assignment.*
- *Above all, spend time with mentees and understand mentoring as a relationship.*

4
Unearth the "Dream"

A seasoned editor with a local newspaper, Mira was known in the community as a wise and caring mentor for a generation of young journalists. When Raphael joined the staff as a new reporter, she began editing his work and showed interest in his career aspirations. Over time, Mira became Raphael's "go-to" source for editing, story ideas, and advice about where to focus his energies and how to maximize his success at the newspaper. As the relationship progressed and Raphael's trust and comfort with Mira increased, he began to offer fragments and glimpses of his "dream" career. Always patient, inquiring, interested, and affirming, Mira was surprised but delighted when she began to understand that Raphael most dearly wished to become a successful fiction writer. Rather than minimize or ridicule Raphael's vision of an ideal life and career, Mira encouraged

him, asked if she could read some of his writing when he felt
ready to share it, and gave him the names of two literary agents
she knew personally.

The renowned sculptor Michelangelo Buonarroti is known to have approached each block of marble with the humble conviction that a sculpture already existed within the stone. For instance, he understood that his sculptures of David and Moses were there all along, merely waiting to be liberated. Michelangelo described sculpting as the art of releasing an ideal figure, already present but hidden from view.

Human beings too possess a unique, promising, but vulnerable inner form. Called the *ideal self* by legendary psychologist Carl Rogers, it represents a person's hopes, aspirations, and dreams. Rogers believed that the ideal self must be revealed and affirmed, or it becomes muted and forgotten. Another luminary in adult development, Daniel Levinson, discovered that young adults often begin to formulate what he termed *the dream*, meaning one's fledgling career and life aspirations. The dream has the quality of a vision or an imagined possibility that generates excitement and vitality in a young person. The dream—like the ideal self—may initially consist of little more than vague wishes or yearnings, including hopes about the skills, traits, and accomplishments one dreams of acquiring. For many people, the dream may be hard to put into words when it lies deep within them.

As you might have already gathered, excellent mentors take heed of Michelangelo's example. Like patient sculptors or archeologists, they watch and listen carefully, always working to gently unearth and then decipher the mentee's ideal self and career dream. They appreciate that their first glimpses of the mentee's dream might not reveal its true nature. Using the tools of attentive listening, unconditional acceptance, Socratic questioning, and generous affirmation, mentors help draw forth the dream, then name it out loud, and, finally, set about helping mentees see what they can indeed attain. In the words of Davis, Little, and Thornton (1997, p. 61), "The mentor nourishes a dream in the mentee and sets the mentee into creative flight, tempering idealism with the wisdom of experience."

Here are two caveats about unearthing the dream. First, there are no shortcuts. The mentor's discernment and affirmation unfolds over time. Unless a mentor heavily invests in the mentee and establishes the trust, a mentee may not feel free to explore and share the contours of the dream. As a consequence, it may never fully become visible to the mentor. Second, humility and modesty are required. Michelangelo modeled these qualities. Keep in mind that unearthing is not about imposing your vision onto mentees but discerning and calling forth to reality what lies within them.

A fascinating stream of research in social psychology called the *Michelangelo Phenomenon* has revealed that in the best relationships, a partner helps to promote the other person's ideal self, which in turn moves the person closer to achieving his or her ideals. A fine mentor helps promote mentees' dreams by (1) seeing mentees as who they imagine themselves becoming, and (2) helping them engage in behaviors aligned with their ideal selves.

Japanese culture provides another way to capture the meaning of this element. The term *sensei* refers to a person born before another and, by implication, someone with greater life experience. But an *onshi* refers to one who gives blessings. Remember that helping to unearth and articulate a mentee's dream is only half of a mentor's mission. The other half involves persistent affirmation and reassurance that the dream is both worthy and attainable. In essence, it is a *blessing*.

KEY COMPONENTS

- *Be vigilant for signs of a mentee's ideal self and career dream.*
- *Listen thoughtfully and give voice to glimpses of the dream.*
- *Like the sculptor Michelangelo, approach your mentee's emerging self with humility.*
- *Once a fledgling life/career dream comes into view, provide copious and persistent doses of affirmation.*

5

Promote Excellence
(but Reject Perfectionism)

As a second-year PhD student in a large psychology program, Cliff began doing research under the supervision of Dr. Wright, an eminent scholar in Cliff's area of interest. From the outset, Dr. Wright was supportive and encouraging but simultaneously challenging. He made it clear to Cliff early on that he would only support Cliff to present and publish work that was exceptionally well conceived and painstakingly polished. When Cliff's work fell short of that expectation, Dr. Wright pulled him aside and said, "Cliff, I'm not here to do mediocre work and neither are you. This work is not indicative of the scholar I know you to be. Try it again." Although sometimes he was annoyed or disheartened by his mentor's stringent requirements, Cliff was about to establish an impressive track record of publications in his field. Upon earning his doctorate and beginning his career as a newly minted psychologist, he was surprised to discover how much he had internalized his mentor's work ethic. Cliff himself became known as an exacting and careful researcher, and this reputation paid off in the form of marked success in grant funding and scholarly publication.

No one starts out in life as a gold medalist, not even an exceptional athlete who has an abundance of natural talent. An athlete develops into a superstar through hard work and practice. The same is true of top performers in every field. But excellence must also be expected. How do mentors set expectations of excellence? And how does a mentor help mentees differentiate excellence from perfection? There are several crucial steps in generating excellence without disheartening or overwhelming mentees.

First, mentors never settle for mediocrity. People tend to perform at the level of their own internalized standards. Often they settle for less. Settling for mediocrity undermines performance because it lowers expectations. Paradoxically, most people are more capable than they think. They need a change in expectations. Here is an important rule: Mentors should expect more of their mentees than their mentees typically expect of themselves. This raises their expectations and lifts their performance.

Second, mentors communicate expectations for excellence. Research on parenting, supervising, and mentoring consistently shows that juniors rise to meet the expectations of mentors—particularly when the mentorship is characterized by trust, support, and mutual respect. Mentors provide a strong sense of inspirational motivation. They communicate high performance expectations through two salient channels. They first model confidence, competence, professionalism, and strong adherence to standards of excellence. They understand the importance of asking of others only what they first ask of themselves. By demanding excellence of themselves, they indirectly but resoundingly voice their high expectations of their mentees.

Then they directly verbalize their high expectations to mentees. They simultaneously communicate unwavering confidence in the mentee's capacity for meeting and even exceeding expectations. Even the most gifted mentee may, at times, lack confidence in some areas, performing only to the level of his or her modest expectations. This all can change when the mentor provides a vision of the mentee as talented, competent, and capable of high-level achievement.

What makes mentors ineffective in exacting expectations? Mentors can fail their mentees in three notable ways. These mistakes undermine the ability of mentees to realize their potential, and neither the mentee nor mentor reaps maximal returns. First, mentors may set their expectations too low. Low expectations fail to challenge mentees to be the best they can be. Although mentors may be kind, caring, and have good intentions, the net effect of their modest requirements is pervasive mediocrity. Only the most self-directed and motivated mentees will thrive when expectations are low.

Second, mentors may make stringent demands for excellence without simultaneously instilling confidence in mentees' capacity to meet these challenges. Without equipment and provisions, mentees are expected to make the journey from neophyte to excellent performer. For the mentee, this is disheartening and undermining. Third, mentors may—intentionally or not—send expectations for perfection (see element 32). Unattainable and destructive, demands for flawless performance sabotage the efforts of the most well-meaning mentor. Unable to reach perfection, mentees can become disenchanted, hopeless, and depressed. Ironically, many excellent mentees are already dangerously perfectionistic. The excellent mentor will detect and refute perfectionism while encouraging excellence and praising approximations to this goal.

KEY COMPONENTS

- *Set high expectations and communicate them clearly.*
- *Model the same excellence you expect from mentees.*
- *Demonstrate confidence in the mentee's capacity to meet your expectations.*
- *Never endorse perfection as a legitimate goal.*

6

Affirm, Affirm, Affirm, and Then Affirm Some More

When Hannah first met Beth at a regional denomination meeting for pastors, she saw a bright, articulate, but somewhat insecure, new pastor. Beth had recently joined a nearby church as the associate pastor and was already struggling with congregational expectations and her own fears about being an "imposter." She perceived herself as ill-suited for the pastoral role. As an accomplished senior pastor, and the only other female pastor in the district, Hannah immediately knew she wanted to mentor Beth. Although she offered Beth numerous practical tips on preaching and inundated her with helpful resources, Hannah soon realized what Beth needed the most— affirmation. One afternoon, looking across her desk at Beth, Hannah said in a firm but caring voice, "Beth, I know you're struggling right now, but hear this: you belong in the pastorate. I've seen you preach, and I know your heart. I believe God meant you to be a pastor. I'm glad you're here." Beth immediately began to sob and then described her parents' disapproval of her career choice and calling to the ministry. During the next several months, Hannah offered strong and unrelenting affirmation. Beth responded with increasing confidence and improved performance. As time went on, Beth's need for con-

*sistent affirmation decreased, and Hannah was able to turn to
more career-oriented issues in mentoring.*

People need to feel good about themselves, and affirmation is
the key to a feeling of well-being. Therefore, the need to be affirmed is human. As Dr. Martin Luther King Jr. once said, "The
only time people do not like praise is when too much of it is
going toward someone else." In young adulthood and early career,
where the stakes are high and the pressure to succeed is intense,
there can be no shortage of affirmation. If you can do only one
thing as a mentor, affirm your mentees.

You can affirm mentees in two ways. You can affirm them as
people. This is the most important type of affirmation. This is an
acknowledgment of a person's inherent worth. Affirming mentees as people should be unconditional and independent of their
performance. You can also affirm mentees as professionals. This is
an acknowledgment of their achievements. Although affirming
mentees as professionals—based upon their performance and
achievement—is important, also ensure that you affirm them as
they make progress in the pursuit of excellence. Withholding
affirmation until goals are achieved is usually a mistake.

Seize every opportunity to give affirmation. But never send
the wrong message that a mentee's worth is contingent on performance. The bottom line is this: affirmation is an artful blend-
ing of personal acceptance and professional endorsement. When
mentors affirm their mentees, they communicate an unequivo-
cal belief in the mentee. When mentees doubt themselves, mentors show confidence in them. When mentees take reasonable
risks, mentors give their approval, and when mentees err, mentors remain serene.

In element 3, we introduced the *imposter syndrome*. Many
mentees suffer this nagging insecurity. On some level, they worry
that if others really knew them, they would not be accepted.

Living in perpetual trepidation that their inadequacies will be discovered, these junior professionals remain inhibited and stunted in their development until affirmed by a mentor. The unflagging faith and confidence of a mentor may have a nearly miraculous effect on a mentee's self-confidence. Excellent mentors provide an affirmation-rich environment where mentees can experiment with their new identities and ride the tumultuous waves that accompany change and growth.

There are two primary components of affirmation. First, affirming mentors communicate and demonstrate faith in the mentee's ability and trust in the mentee's judgment. Research indicates that when mentees feel accepted and confirmed by a mentor, they are more willing to trust the mentor, believe in themselves, and accept increasingly challenging tasks. Affirmed mentees exude confidence. They are assured of acceptance— even when they fail.

The second component is more subtle and demanding of the mentor. Excellent mentors are so tuned in to their mentees that they can discern each one's unique potential. The discernment may cover career and personal potential. We call this *blessing* (see element 4). The astute mentor helps the mentee articulate the dream and then blesses the mentee by affirming that the dream is possible. Of course, mentors must simultaneously temper unrealistic dreams, bringing the wisdom of experience to bear on the mentee's aspirations. Nonetheless, affirming is something every mentor should do.

KEY COMPONENTS
- *Consistently and unconditionally affirm your mentee as a person of great value.*
- *Regularly affirm your mentee's professional performance.*
- *Instill confidence in your mentees to help them overcome self-doubt and the "imposter syndrome."*

- *Seek to discern and then endorse your mentee's life and career "dream." Then work diligently to help him or her achieve it.*
- *Gently shed light on unrealistic aspirations and find ways to affirm mentees even in the face of short-term failure.*

7

Provide Sponsorship

As the principal of a large suburban high school, Burt took notice of Jennifer, one of his brightest and most creative young teachers. Not only was Jennifer a gifted teacher and immensely popular with students and colleagues, she was also ambitious and curious about opportunities in educational leadership. Sensing that Jennifer would benefit from some career assistance, Burt urged her to apply for the district's competitive MA tuition-remission program. He wrote her a stellar letter of recommendation, and within two years Jennifer had completed her master's degree. Burt then recommended her to the superintendent for the very competitive administrative training program (a pipeline for future principals). Along the way, Burt invited Jennifer to some important district meetings where he introduced her to key leadership personnel and got her assigned to some high-profile committees and projects. Within five years, Jennifer took over the principal position at a large high school. Several years later, she became the assistant superintendent of a large neighboring school district.

No one can seize an opportunity if the door is shut. Sometimes mentors can open doors that mentees cannot open for themselves. They can endorse mentees' membership in important organizations, invite them to exclusive meetings, and sponsor them for work on special or high-visibility projects. Mentors may introduce mentees to important individuals in the organization or in their profession. Mentors can help promising mentees make presentations at conferences or participate in important meetings. Studies of distinguished (Nobel Prize–winning) scientists show that sponsorship is often a critical component of gaining eminence in one's career. Successful scientists often study under leading researchers and, in turn, sponsor rising stars in the sciences.

Sponsorship carries with it a sharing of power and social capital in a profession or organization. As the mentee is associated with the mentor and the mentor endorses the mentee's work, others accord the mentee *reflective power*—power of the mentor by extension. Reflective power can melt barriers, open doors, and provide access to influential people who normally would not be accessible to a mentee. The mentor's reflective power can be thought of as a sort of mentee shield. This shield, bearing the mentor's coat of arms, communicates to others in the professional context that the mentee has the backing, support, and promotion of a person of prominence.

Like the other skill-based elements of mentoring, effective sponsorship requires thoughtful intention. Accurate sponsorship demands familiarity with a mentee's specific career aspirations. Mentors must tailor sponsorship efforts to the mentee's unique life dream. Familiarity with a mentee's personal dream should help the mentor select organizations, meetings, committees, and other uniquely targeted opportunities for the mentee. You might consider this "precision sponsorship."

The most effective sponsors are raving fans of their mentees. When opportunities arise, they praise their mentees in public, talk up their achievements to key stakeholders in the organization, and go out of the way to connect them to known influencers in their own network of colleagues and acquaintances. The best mentors are assertive and vocal about a mentee's achievements and future potential.

Sponsorship allows a fledgling professional to try new behaviors and hone the skills needed for success in any organization. This is critical for early career success, and it could make the difference in how mentees advance professionally. Make no mistake, though, that with sponsorship comes risk. Poor performance by a sponsored mentee could negatively impact the mentor's stature and ultimately the ability to provide sponsorship in the future. It behooves mentors to take the necessary precautions to prevent such an outcome. Mastering all of the elements in this book is a good prevention strategy.

KEY COMPONENTS

- *Discern your mentee's unique career dream.*
- *Consider which opportunities (e.g., committees, organizations, projects, professional experiences) would best prepare the mentee to achieve this dream.*
- *Use your status and influence to help the mentee gain entry to groups and experiences that could be career enhancing.*
- *Allow the mentee to serve as your emissary at times—shielded by your reflective power and functioning on your behalf.*
- *Be a vocal raving fan of your mentee so that others take notice of him or her.*

8

Actively Teach and Coach

Although he was only four years Jim's senior in the company and only a couple of years older, Noel quickly became one of Jim's most important career mentors. The mentorship formed when Jim became a management trainee. A relatively junior manager himself, Noel had established himself as a productive and well-liked member of the company. He quickly saw Jim as bright and promising and took him under his tutelage. He advised Jim about how he should present himself, who he should get to know, and who he should avoid. He guided Jim on several difficult projects, pointing out the critical components and carefully teaching him the process. Noel helped him to prepare for important meetings and presentations, cautioning him regarding common mistakes. When Jim succeeded, Noel celebrated. When Jim fell short of expectations, Noel helped him to learn from the experience and move on.

If you teach effectively, mentees will learn. Take time to give direct and explicit instruction. Excellent mentors provide knowledge, make recommendations, offer consultation, and stimulate motivation with encouragement. Their broad perspectives and experiences in the field make them attractive to potential mentees.

It is not surprising that the obituaries of highly regarded educators often highlight their profound gifts as mentors. They have likely guided generations of student mentees. Nor is it surprising that great mentors are frequently described as patient and effective teachers. No matter the field of study, the nature of the discipline, or the characteristics of the mentee, good mentoring requires good teaching. We began this book with the words of Sophocles: "The reasonable thing is to learn from those who can teach." Quite frankly, if you have nothing to teach, or if you are unable to teach what you know, then do not presume to mentor. Mentees are drawn to those who teach: individuals who deliberately instruct and demonstrate the salient behaviors of a seasoned master in the mentee's field of interest.

Teaching often takes the form of direct training and information sharing. Mentors bolster a mentee's technical competence by providing knowledge and refining specific professional skills. Excellent mentors are eager and invested teachers. In contrast to the reluctant guru who occasionally rewards the dogged seeker with small nuggets of wisdom, the outstanding mentor creates opportunities to give advice, recount relevant experiences, and provide consultation on challenges that lie ahead. Good mentors are inherently educators. They understand that learning is a catalyst to growth.

Although most teaching is explicit, mentees also benefit from vicarious instruction that occurs through mentor storytelling. Some mentors are particularly effective at informally transferring knowledge about the workplace. Self-disclosure in the service of self-adulation or selfish catharsis is nearly always counterproductive. At times, salient lessons about life and career are best communicated by sharing one's personal stories of tribulation and triumph. But keep this principle in mind: self-disclosure is an adjunct to, not a substitute for, overt and direct forms of teaching.

Mentors provide mentees with crucial insider information, but they avoid gossip. Through their teaching, they cover a range of topics. They instruct mentees about the subtleties of local politics and organizational power. Good mentors teach mentees strategies for managing conflict and coach them on setting short- and long-term goals. Also, they teach mentees the norms that set the acceptable range of behaviors.

Finally, good mentors understand when it is helpful to use a particular instructional strategy. Although the sharing of direct advice and instruction may be particularly important early in the mentorship, mentees may require less direct information-giving and teaching as the relationship matures. As mentees become increasingly confident and competent, they may operate with more independence. Therefore, teaching should be most active early in the mentoring but continue to some degree throughout the process.

KEY COMPONENTS

- *Give direct and explicit instruction on the various roles and functions required in your vocation.*
- *Intentionally demonstrate and describe complex professional skills.*
- *Seize opportunities for training and instruction through personal example and storytelling.*
- *Gradually decrease the amount of direct teaching as mentees develop and succeed.*

9

Encourage and Support

When Nancy landed a slot in an extremely competitive university doctoral program, she wondered if she had somehow slipped in by mistake. A divorced mother of three and a mid-career student, she wondered if she really "belonged" in graduate school. Although her mentor, Dr. Abrams, had selected Nancy largely due to her extremely high test scores and skillful writing ability, Nancy continued to doubt her own potential. During the first two years of the mentorship, Dr. Abrams recognized Nancy's self-doubt and therefore gave her strong and consistent encouragement and support. Not only did Dr. Abrams listen intently to Nancy's concerns about balancing the roles of mother and student, he often reminded her that she was selected into the program because she was exceptionally talented and someone he expected to be successful. So consistent was Dr. Abrams's encouragement and support, Nancy began to see herself through his positive and confident lens.

You may not master all the skills of mentoring, but chances are mentees will appreciate your efforts if you encourage them and provide them with emotional support. Famous psychologist Carl Rogers theorized that for growth to occur in counseling, a counselor needs to be kind, warm, and willing to offer unconditional positive regard to clients. In his opinion, specific counseling techniques and therapeutic procedures were less important than basic warmth and acceptance. Indeed, decades of research on helping relationships (counseling, psychotherapy, and mentoring) confirm his theory. People thrive when they feel safe, valued, and well supported. When a mentor is friendly, open, approachable, and consistently encouraging, mentees are more at ease with risk-taking, more assured that they can succeed, and more comfortable asking for advice and assistance.

Encouragement and support are always valuable. But there are times when they are especially necessary. Beginners in any field often experience the anxiety that accompanies facing new challenges. Other mentees encounter difficult times personally or professionally. Numerous studies, across a range of professions and mentoring contexts, find that encouragement and support are among the most important mentoring functions.

Here is a word of caution: Although encouragement and support may seem easy to give, they often are not. In fact, these skills may be difficult to learn. Like new counselors struggling to master the seemingly simple subtleties of genuine warmth and accurate listening, mentors may struggle with the fine art of encouragement and support. The greatest struggle may be with a mentee who is bright and self-confident. Mentors may assume erroneously that these individuals do not need that type of encouragement. But their assumption may be dead wrong. Then there are mentors who are too busy to lend emotional support, while still others may be uncomfortable in the encourager role. For whatever reason, failure to encourage and support diminishes the strength and value of the mentorship.

Encouragement and support are necessary throughout a mentoring relationship. They are especially crucial early in the mentorship when the relationship between mentor and mentee is beginning to develop. But it does not stop there. Mentors should seize every opportunity to speak a kind word, lift a mentee's spirit, encourage a mentee to stay the course, and be a sounding board when there is a need. The importance of encouragement and support cannot be overstated. Research consistently shows that mentees appreciate mentors who display these qualities and criticize those who do not.

KEY COMPONENTS

- *Expect even the most talented and confident mentee to benefit from encouragement and support.*
- *Understand that while foundational to mentoring, encouragement and support are not easy to practice.*
- *Seek opportunities to offer support, praise, and encouragement.*
- *Supportive mentors are genuine, consistent, warm, and accepting.*

10

Shape New Behaviors

Fresh from radiology technician school, Rachel appeared more uncomfortable in her new job than any tech Donna had encountered. A seasoned radiology clinic supervisor with a penchant for mentoring, Donna quickly discerned that Rachel had little self-confidence. She had trouble making eye contact with patients and was reluctant to conduct x-rays without constant supervision. Sensing the heart of the problem, Donna pulled Rachel aside and encouraged her to take time developing rap-

port with patients. She also asked her to try completing a few x-ray series without direct oversight. Then, Donna watched Rachel like a hawk. When Donna saw Rachel make small forays into small talk with patients or offer slightly more eye contact, she was quick to praise her for it. When Rachel completed her first radiology series alone, Donna surprised her with a big grin and a hug. Donna observed that Rachel was most responsive to encouraging words and moral support, so each time Rachel took an interpersonal risk, demonstrated initiative, or worked independently, Donna was quick with a smile, a wink, and an affirmative comment. Each comment was about Rachel's professionalism and her potential as "radiology star." In short order, Rachel blossomed under the light of Donna's reinforcing gaze.

Behavioral psychologist B. F. Skinner discovered that behavior can be gradually changed through the use of reinforcement. His technique entailed what he called *successive approximations* (element 10). As the behavior of subjects in his studies more closely approximated the desired behavior, Skinner would reinforce the behavior by giving them something tangible. Using this technique, he had great success increasing desirable behavior. For instance, he was able to teach pigeons to play ping-pong.

To effectively shape behavior, begin with what you have. In mentoring, start with the initial skills, mindset, attitudes, and experiences of the mentee. Every mentee is different. So you have to make an assessment of each one, determining the individual's initial capacity. Next identify the reinforcers that work best for each individual. One thing is for certain: praise is preferable to punishment. For instance, children are more responsive to parental accolades and tangible rewards than to demeaning words or spankings. Managers get more mileage out of subordinates' performance by giving them incentives and plaques than from public humiliation or threats. And mentors unleash maximum mentee growth and achievement through the judicious use of well-timed reinforcement.

How do mentors use reinforcement to shape mentees? When a mentee makes a fledgling effort at a novel task, takes a risk, or shows slight improvement in some area of performance, the attentive mentor is quick to deliver a well-matched reinforcement. Depending on the mentee and the context, an appropriate reinforcement may include a proud smile, a fist bump, verbal praise, a public announcement, or an invitation to assume a larger role in some project. Of course, knowing your mentees entails learning which reinforcers are most salient for them. Effective mentors tailor their reinforcement patterns to fit each mentee's developmental level and predilections for certain reinforcers.

Here is the tough part: waiting until a mentee masters a skill set or performs a task at a level expected of professionals before delivering reinforcement is unwise. Instead, the savvy mentor reinforces each successive approximation to the desired goal. As the mentee makes increasingly accurate or effective approximations to the desired behavior (e.g., cogent writing, clear verbal communication, a major sale), the mentor is quick to deliver reinforcement at each milestone along the way. Each sign of progress or improvement should naturally elicit some approving and encouraging response for the mentor.

So what's wrong with punishment? Applying noxious stimuli to decrease the frequency of unwanted behavior is an age-old endeavor. We have all seen supervisors make humiliating digs, deliver icy glares, threaten termination, or give the silent treatment. Punishment is ineffective as a major tool of mentoring because it simply suppresses unwanted behavior. Unlike reinforcement, punishment fails to teach mentees new behavior. In addition, punishment is notorious for its unintended side effects, such as physical or emotional harm, stress, fear, and diminished hope.

Consider the infamous *learned helplessness* experiment conducted by psychologist Martin Seligman (Seligman & Maier, 1967). When Seligman applied random and unpleasant electrical shocks to dogs that were harnessed inside a box, they rather quickly stopped struggling, recognizing that the punishment was inescapable. These same dogs were then placed—unharnessed—in a modified box from which they could easily jump over a small partition and walk away. They did not. These conditioned—and now depressed—canines simply lay on the ground whimpering as the shocks commenced. Punishment had created a state of helplessness and hopelessness. Seligman's dogs behaved as though their efforts would not effect change.

Use praise as a developmental tool. Deliberately shape protégé behavior using methods of reinforcement suited to them. And avoid punishment. Learned helplessness will never allow your mentees to achieve desired outcomes.

KEY COMPONENTS
- *Deliberately reinforce evidence of growth and improvement.*
- *Remember: no two mentees begin at the same starting point.*
- *Intentionally shape closer and closer approximations to the end goal.*
- *Take time to discern what is most reinforcing for your mentee.*
- *Beware of the unintended consequences of punishment.*

11

Offer Counsel in Difficult Times

As a vice president in a nonprofit educational consulting organization, Dan was in a position to mentor a number of junior professionals. Derek was one of Dan's primary mentees. He benefited enormously from Dan's steady career advice, guidance, and support. In the second year of the mentorship, Derek went through a painful divorce. He turned to Dan with questions about his own competence, the organization's view of his personal problems, and even questions about whether his devotion to work had sabotaged his marriage. Although Dan did not try to play the role of a psychologist, he did advise Derek to worry less about the job, place a priority on his self-care, and avoid making significant career decisions in his current state of mind. He assured Derek that what others in the organization thought about his personal life would not be allowed to hamper his job security as long as he continued his excellent track record. Throughout the hardest phase of Derek's divorce, Dan counseled patience, self-care, and perspective-taking.

Mentoring is not professional counseling or therapy. But sooner or later, a mentee will ask for a mentor's wise counsel on a personal concern. Mentorships often occur during a phase of the mentee's life characterized by stress, change, and growing pains. Therefore, it is not surprising that mentorships occasionally include a dimension best described as informal counseling. Mentees benefit from discussing their problems with their mentor and exploring possible solutions. Most mentee concerns and difficulties can be clustered into three broad domains—developing professional competence and career satisfaction, managing professional relationships, and managing the competing demands of one's career and personal life.

Concerns bearing on competence and career satisfaction typically take the form of either perceived inadequacy—the imposter syndrome—or doubt about the extent of a match between mentee and career track. Buffeted by overwhelming demands, insecurity, or unsavory glimpses at the real life of the professional, mentees may experience the rise of their emotional needs to the surface. They may want reassurance that they can succeed. They may want advice on how to navigate their career trajectories. They may want permission to reconsider their career choice and to do so without the threat of reprisal or ridicule.

Concerns bearing on professional relationships take many forms. They may involve the management of interactions with difficult colleagues or supervisors. Take a mentee who seeks advice about handling a supervisor's unreasonable demands, hostility, an unfair evaluation, or inappropriate sexual overtures. In these types of situations, the mentor has to exercise great wisdom. When counseling in these situations, the mentor must be discreet and supportive—helping without parenting and protecting without smothering the mentee. Sometimes wise counsel will require direct confrontation. Even excellent mentees commit snafus or exacerbate relational problems with colleagues, which means these behaviors need to be pointed out and mandated to change.

Concerns regarding the management of career and other facets of mentees' personal lives are plentiful. Juggling multiple roles—such as junior professional, spouse, parent, child, and member of a community—is common. In these various roles, mentees struggle with the stress of balancing their responsibilities and fragmented identities. They need guidance in how to be successful in each of their roles without compromising themselves in any one role.

How do mentors offer counsel? First, they should recognize their limitations and never pretend to be professional counselors. For example, mentors should not expect themselves to be able to help mentees with all of their problems, nor should they attempt to treat obvious mental health problems. Clearly, problems like severe depression or substance abuse disorders are out of the league of most mentors. When they encounter serious problems such as these, they should encourage the mentee to get professional care. Even when mentors themselves are mental health professionals, they must be ethical. They should maintain their boundaries, avoid a dual relationship, and refer the mentee to another professional.

Second, although they are not counseling professionals, mentors allow mentees to explore both personal and professional issues in the context of the mentorship. Skills such as active listening, accurate understanding of and reflecting feelings, clarifying strategies for making decisions, and assisting in the setting of goals may help mentees to accept and overcome inner doubts and personal obstacles. Moreover, mentors should convey acceptance, normalize the existence of problems and distress, and facilitate problem-solving. Mentees are profoundly helped by the mere willingness of the mentor to listen to and validate their concerns. Confident mentors are comfortable with providing emotional triage—calm listening, empathy, encouragement, and immediate problem-solving in the context of personal or vocational emergencies in the lives of mentees without allowing the mentorship to become a professional counseling relationship.

Third, mentors should not avoid the responsibility of offering wise counsel. They understand that offering counsel is inevitable in mentoring, that it may enhance the mentoring relationship, and that wise counsel can facilitate a mentee's personal and professional development.

Finally, mentors should discourage mentees from trying to use the mentorship for professional counseling or psychotherapy. This is a misuse of the relationship that carries serious negative consequences. It can damage the relationship and lead to counterproductive outcomes. Therefore, mentors need to exercise discretion regarding the limits of their counseling. At the same time, they need to help mentees maintain their boundaries between mentorship and therapy-seeking.

KEY COMPONENTS

- *Be open to discussing and exploring mentee concerns and difficulties.*
- *Actively listen, reflect feelings, and clarify alternatives.*
- *Offer unconditional acceptance and validate the mentee's experience.*
- *Accept your limitations; refer mentees to a professional when serious emotional disturbance emerges.*

12

Protect as Necessary

As a first-year resident in a competitive neurology residency program, Dr. Emily Myers came under the tutelage of Dr. Maria Chavez, her primary rotation supervisor and a senior member of the medical staff. Although Emily was an outstanding physician, she was somewhat eccentric and socially inept. Unbeknownst to Emily, she was often the brunt of behind-the-back teasing from other residents. Nonetheless, Dr. Chavez saw Emily as a talented young physician. She noticed that Emily's social eccentricities seemed to be lessening as her confidence and competence increased. During a faculty meeting to evaluate residents, several junior male members of the faculty began mimicking Emily's odd dress and habits. Dr. Chavez recognized this sabotaging behavior as the kind of thing that could easily undermine a resident's status in the program. She calmly but sternly stated, "The last time I checked, gentlemen, fashionable dress and social grace were not evaluation criterion in our residency. Dr. Myers is one of my most promising residents. I hope that in the future you will limit your comments and observations to relevant concerns." That statement sent a clear message to the training faculty. Emily enjoyed the support and protection of her mentor. Although Emily became a successful graduate of the residency, she was never aware of her mentor's protective intervention.

The road to success can be lined with perils and danger. Some are obvious. Others are less so. Sometimes even the most talented mentee can be blindsided by obstacles along the road to success. Because mentors have traveled a similar road, they are more familiar with the signs of danger and should be prepared to protect their mentees. Occasionally, the mentor must don armor, shield, and sword to discourage or repel an inappropriate attack.

Career threats take on many forms—bureaucratic entanglements, conflict with colleagues, hostile criticism, assignment to tasks likely to sabotage success, and one's own poor judgment. A mentor who fails to respond expeditiously to such threats renders the mentee vulnerable to a range of negative outcomes—including career failure. When a mentee is threatened, mentor protection becomes crucial. Just like threats, protection may take many forms. Mentors may publicly advocate for the mentee, directly confront hostile parties (or their supervisors), create shortcuts through bureaucratic red tape, and prevent the assignment of the mentee to either low-visibility roles or roles that are likely to overwhelm the mentee.

Effective protection demands calm and measured assertiveness. The credible mentor is deliberate but thoughtful in coming to the rescue of the mentee. Signs of outrage, indignation, and personal disturbance diminish the mentor's credibility. These signs telegraph either excess ego-involvement in the mentee or an arrogant stance that no one should "dare" challenge or mistreat the mentor's affiliates. In either case, the mentor loses, coupled with an inability to protect the mentee.

Protection, however, can be a double-edged sword. Overprotection, even to the extent of bullying others on behalf of the mentee, is often tantamount to turning a blind eye when a mentee may have real problems in performance. Sometimes it is simply better for mentors to confront their mentees than spare them the experience of hurt feelings. Whenever overprotective mentors fail to acknowledge mentees' weaknesses and failures, they lose power and credibility. Instead of garnering admiration, they are seen as an unreasonable avenger. Therefore, while it is essential to protect mentees from the incursion of unjustifiable threats, it is equally important to confront them for unacceptable performance. Just as failure to protect a mentee may damage his or her professional identity and career, excessive or misinformed efforts at protection may undermine mentee autonomy and sabotage the mentor's credibility.

KEY COMPONENTS

- *Accept the fact that mentees will occasionally suffer career-inhibiting personal or political attacks.*
- *Respond expeditiously but calmly to unfair threats or attacks against a mentee; avoid the appearance of rage or indignation.*

- *Use protection sparingly; frequent intervention reduces mentor credibility.*
- *Honestly consider mentee contributions to professional conflicts.*
- *Never bully anyone.*

13

Stimulate Growth with Challenging Assignments

When Charlie assumed duties as the new assistant vice president for human resources, he developed a profound respect for Doug. Doug was his immediate boss and the vice president of the human resources division. Doug also was a remarkably accomplished speaker and motivator; he was well known in the company and in the larger training community for his leadership-development workshops. Doug immediately began to mentor Charlie. He provided direct teaching and coaching in the art of training, praised Charlie's early efforts, and pushed him to take an increasing role in the weekly workshops. Although initially terrified of being the "upfront" man, Charlie found not only that he survived each new challenge but that he actually enjoyed himself. Several months later, with Charlie feeling reasonably confident in the presenter role, Doug announced to Charlie that it was time for Charlie to start "taking the reins." Doug had scheduled Charlie as the main speaker for an important executive leadership workshop in another city. Although Charlie was initially terrified, Doug reassured him that he was ready and noted, "I told them they were getting one of our best trainers." Charlie was well received, and his confidence was bolstered.

Change, the kind that shows positive transformation, typically comes about through a deliberate process. Normally it does not take place overnight. Nor does it occur with one try. Mentee growth and development, for instance, are catalyzed when mentors create progressively more challenging assignments. Mentee competence and confidence are likely to increase at a commensurate rate at which the mentor provides challenges. The assignment of challenging work is essential for both technical skill development and professional identity enhancement. Maximally useful assignments must be accompanied by both critical feedback and reinforcing praise.

Skillful mentors tailor assignments to the needs of mentees. They attempt to facilitate growth and development without overwhelming the mentee or inducing unwarranted failure. Here are three relevant guidelines.

First, shape performance through successive approximations. To shape means to improve gradually, to move someone closer to the expected performance. Incrementally more difficult assignments result in growth as long as the immediate expectations do not supersede the mentee's current level of ability. Therefore, find the optimal beginning point for each mentee, and then shape according to the mentee's pace of development. Aim high. But do not start too high or too low. Furthermore, do not shape too fast or too slow. Above all, look for the right balance for each mentee.

Second, find the right challenge for your mentee. Regardless of your profession or work setting, each mentee is an individual. Each will present a unique blend of talents, interests, and personal qualities. Find progressively demanding jobs that match each mentee. For instance, two mentees may have similar backgrounds and experience; one may be introverted and socially phobic (though precise in written communication), while the other may be outgoing and comedic (though prone to neglect attention to detail). These mentees require different challenges for maximal growth. While honoring each mentee's gifts, the challenging mentor will give assignments that are individually stretching.

Third, help mentees manage their anxiety. Performance anxiety comes with the territory of growth and development. Depending on how it is managed, anxiety can hinder or enhance the developing mentee. Teach mentees that anxiety is normal; in fact, anxiety is ubiquitous to the human experience. Encourage mentees to use anxiety as a source of motivation. Assist mentees in understanding that moderate anxiety can help them clear new hurdles of performance. And help mentees to recognize that the absence of anxiety can compromise good motivation. Ultimately, there is no cure for anxiety apart from direct and repeated exposure to the anxiety-evoking situation. Excellent mentors use good humor, patience, and firm persistence in challenging mentees to walk toward—not away from—opportunities and tasks that create some anxiety.

KEY COMPONENTS

- *Deliberately challenge mentees with demanding assignments tailored to their abilities and performance thresholds.*
- *Shape performance through successive approximations to the desired goal.*
- *Avoid making demands that exceed mentee performance capacities.*
- *Help mentees accept, tolerate, and effectively manage anxiety in the face of new challenges.*
- *Remember, repeated and direct exposure is the only cure for anxiety.*

14

Give Mentees Exposure and Promote Their Visibility

Fresh out of college, Stuart began writing ad copy for some of the smallest accounts in a large Los Angeles advertisement firm. On several occasions, Marsha, the firm's creative director, came to Stuart with last-minute "emergency" jobs. In each instance, Stuart worked long hours, did excellent work, and even helped Marsha fine-tune the client presentation. Very impressed with Stuart's ability and work ethic, Marsha began grooming him for a larger role in the firm. Specifically, she began shunting some high-profile client projects Stuart's way, paired him with one of the more successful artists in the firm, and began mentioning Stuart's successes to the other directors and partners. While careful not to overwhelm him, Marsha selected clients and projects that were especially well matched with Stuart's interests and strengths—helping ensure further success. Marsha made sure that clients would take note of Stuart's accomplishments, and many of them began to insist that Stuart direct their accounts. As Stuart's successes mounted, Marsha mentioned him frequently as a potential future director in the firm.

Trumpet your mentee's successes and expose them to the senior leaders in the organization. Organizational research shows that a salient component of early career socialization is the opportunity for junior professionals to demonstrate competence to others. As mentors expose mentees to new responsibilities and create individually tailored challenges, they simultaneously must seek out or create opportunities for public exposure. Outstanding mentors draw attention to their mentees by highlighting their contributions and achievements both laterally (to peers and colleagues) and vertically (to superiors). Of course, mentors must keep their egos in check as well as feel secure within themselves. Otherwise, they will be threatened by the accolades and praise not coming their way.

The best way to generate visibility for mentees is to give them high-profile assignments. Working on important accounts, participating on influential committees, or landing a project that requires considerable interface with influential stakeholders are all excellent methods of enhancing positive exposure. Certainly, mentors must make sure mentees are prepared to meet the challenge. Otherwise, failure in high-visibility assignments can shake a mentee's confidence or ruin a mentor's credibility. Failure may also derail a mentee's opportunities for advancement. Mentees need the good judgment of the mentor to assure them that they are ready for the challenge, and they also need to trust that the mentor's judgment is sound.

We recommend creating initial exposure and visibility via collaborative efforts with mentees. In the world of academe, mentors can co-author articles, team-teach, and co-present conference papers with graduate students or junior faculty. In business organizations, mentors can create subprojects and collateral tasks suited to the person's talent and experience. These collaborations offer the mentee credibility by association without incurring substantial risk. As mentee successes accrue, the mentor makes them public and searches for other opportunities for the mentee to build on them.

KEY COMPONENTS

- *Draw attention to mentees by highlighting their achievements to both your colleagues and superiors.*
- *Create opportunities for mentee collaboration on high-visibility projects.*

- *Promote positive mentee interface with influential stake-holders.*
- *Ensure that mentee successes and achievements are made visible within the organization.*

15

Nurture Creativity

Nearing retirement, Dr. Smith was delighted when Javier, a newly minted doctorate, accepted an assistant professorship at his college. As chair of the college's small psychology department, Dr. Smith had watched enrollment in psychology courses steadily decline over the last decade. Things changed dramatically during Javier's first year on the job when students began excitedly mentioning the "strange" new professor's classroom antics. Rather than lecture constantly as was the custom in the department, Javier repeatedly arranged for unconventional events to occur in his social psychology class. He also appeared in the dress and character of famous psychologists in his history of psychology class and had students act the part of disordered clients in his abnormal psychology class. In the classroom, Javier was energetic, challenging, unpredictable, and given to imaginative role-play and in-class demonstration. Although enrollment in psychology courses and interest in the psychology major swelled, some professors in the department were put off by Javier's unconventional approach. Nonetheless, Dr. Smith praised Javier's creativity, trumpeted his teaching excellence to the college dean, and encouraged Javier to write about his teaching ideas. Not only did Javier advance rapidly, he became a nationally known author on the topic of innovative teaching techniques. He eventually became dean of instruction at a major university.

Everyone has something special and unique to offer. For some people, the uniqueness is more obvious than for others. Nevertheless, mentors should attempt to awaken the creativity and innovation that each mentee possesses. They should nurture their mentees' dreams and help them realize their special potentialities. Extensive research programs with children suggest that having a mentor correlates significantly with various measures of adult creative achievement. Sponsors or patrons nourish independence and creativity while intervening in the social system to prevent tradition, inertia, and inflexibility from hampering mentee creativity. In this mentoring context, originality is endorsed, and this often persists as an aspect of the mentee's adult professional identity.

The role of a mentor in nurturing creativity is analogous to the actions of a midwife. A mentor offers a protective sanctuary in which creativity is first recognized and encouraged. As mentees take risks or generate new ideas and innovative strategies, mentors applaud these efforts. They listen sincerely to tentative proposals and ideas, and they ardently resist opportunities to ridicule and reject. Nurturing creativity also requires the mentor to temper idealism and dreamful expansiveness with the wisdom of experience and the discipline of reality. This is a difficult dance, for no one really knows another person's ultimate potential. But outstanding mentors err on the side of being flexible and affirming, especially when mentees are just getting started, and their creative potential is still unknown.

Who is better suited than a mentor to nurture creativity? Mentors themselves typically are creative. They model creativity by pursuing unusual solutions to problems, questioning accepted standards in the field, and displaying energetic excitement in the face of challenge. They are firsthand exemplars.

KEY COMPONENTS

- *Encourage innovative thought and creative problem-solving in mentees.*
- *Provide a safe haven for creative mentees to develop and experiment with novel approaches.*
- *Reinforce creativity while tempering overexpansiveness with reality and pragmatics.*
- *Model innovation and creative excitement for mentees.*

16

Provide Correction—Even When Painful

Ingrid had mentored Dana as a manager for a year. Dana, in many respects, was competent, creative, and savvy. Well-liked by customers, peers, and managers, Dana had only a couple of discernable shortcomings. She tended to complete tasks at the last minute, and her preparation for major presentations was spotty. When confronted, she would gloss over the feedback with charm and humor. As a result, Ingrid expressed some serious reservations to Dana about the long-term impact of this behavior on her career and future with the company. Following a particularly disorganized presentation, Ingrid confronted Dana more forcefully than ever: "Dana, your presentation today was poorly prepared and unprofessional. It fell far below the level of excellence I would expect from someone with your talent. Not only are you doing yourself a disservice, your substandard work is beginning to reflect unfavorably on me. In order to continue as your champion in the company, I need to see a dramatic turnaround in your planning and preparation."

No one is perfect. That's why even the sharpest mentee can benefit from constructive criticism. Failing to offer correction when it is needed is a disservice to the mentee. This omission reflects the mentor's incompetence, disinterest, or avoidance of conflict. Good mentors address subpar performance and lack of attention to detail. They offer critical but constructive appraisals and point out strategies for mentees to overcome their shortcomings. Although it's important to encourage creativity and innovation, mentors must simultaneously shine the light of realism and feasibility on enthusiastic (but sometimes unrealistic) mentee plans.

In providing correction, timing is everything. Critical reflection and performance feedback are most palatable and useful to the mentee who has gone through the initial phase of mentorship. Personal insecurity becomes less troubling, and confidence begins to take form. The mentor is sensitive to the mentee's level of development, tempering criticism with an appreciation of the mentee's confidence and capacity for constructive response to correction. Early in the mentorship, effective correction should be preceded by a healthy dose of affirmation and encouragement. As a mentorship seasons and mentees develop, confrontation may become more direct, less buffered, and the mentee should not feel as threatened as he or she would without the seasoning and development. In addition to performance-based correction, mentors also must be willing to address unethical or unprofessional mentee behavior. Mentees vary in their understanding of what is ethically acceptable or in their commitment to behave ethically. In an effort to achieve rapid success, the overzealous mentee may cut ethical corners, such as lying or taking credit for work done by others. In confronting a mentee's unethical behavior, mentors offer an essential service to the profession and to the mentee. The reputation of the profession is spared, as are serious consequences for the mentee.

Mentors also should be attuned to the mentee's personal health. They can help mentees address unhealthy work habits (e.g., compulsive overworking, social isolation, pervasive conflict with coworkers) and evidence of personal distress (e.g., depression, anxiety, chronic anger). They can help mentees realize that problem work habits interfere with both long-term health and career success. Mentors should understand that dysfunctional work habits and personal distress can emanate from one of two primary sources. *State disturbances* are situational; the mentee is impacted or overwhelmed by circumstances, cumulative stress, or on-the-job events. State disturbances are transient, making a good prognosis for constructive change. *Trait disturbances*, conversely, are characterological; they are rooted in the very foundation of the mentee's personality. Although trait disturbances (e.g., compulsivity, pervasive self-doubt, volatile anger) must be confronted, they are more difficult to change than state disturbances. Mentors need a potent intervention that may require the assistance of a neutral health professional or executive coach.

Finally, confrontation can be paradoxical. On the one hand, confronting a mentee may surface some pain, but it shows caring. On the other hand, avoiding a confrontation may spare the mentee some pain but causes greater vulnerability to costly errors and unchecked dysfunction. Mentors who really care confront problem behavior.

KEY COMPONENTS

- *Confront self-defeating, unprofessional, or career-inhibiting mentee behavior.*
- *Temper confrontation with realistic affirmation—especially early on.*
- *Quickly address unethical, unprofessional, and illegal mentee behavior.*

- *Kindly confront personal distress and sabotaging work habits without assuming a mental health practitioner role.*
- *Recognize that appropriate confrontation builds trust.*

17

Give the Inside Scoop

Right off the bat, Andrea noticed both Katie's work and her work ethic. A recent college graduate, Katie had impressed her internship supervisor so much that she had landed a coveted managerial-track job in a large financial management company. As one of the more senior women managers in the division, Andrea was committed to mentoring several of the most promising female hires each year to help increase the success and retention of women in the company. A solid mentorship quickly formed, and mutual trust and respect between the two ensued. Out of concern for her mentee, Andrea began to slowly impart key bits of information and advice, both about the firm and about career success as a female manager. For instance, she told Katie about several women predecessors who had failed and explained why. She helped Katie to understand the difference between the published criteria for promotion and the subtle or implicit criteria. Andrea also taught Katie about the company's key priorities, cultural values, and traditions, and she coached Katie on what to wear, how to best present herself, and what to say (and not say) in meetings with long-term clients and top executives. By offering the inside perspective and polishing Katie's presentation, Andrea helped her to clear the company's early career hurdles successfully.

All organizations operate off of a set of assumptions, values, norms, patterns of behavior, and tangible artifacts and symbols.

Collectively, these features comprise organizational culture. Edgar Schein, a leading theorist on the subject, asserts that the most important aspects of organizational culture are these fundamental assumptions. Because many assumptions are implicit, newcomers may not realize their importance when navigating through organizations. Understanding the fundamental assumptions and values of an organization's culture can mean the difference between success and failure.

One of the most valuable but rarely discussed elements of mentorship is the practice of conveying wisdom that only a system insider, often a seasoned veteran, can pass along. When mentors socialize their mentees, they provide crucial insider information about an organization or a profession, convey the implicit values and subtle skills that cumulatively make one a professional, and burnish the behaviors and competencies other professionals expect from one of their own.

New members of any profession or organization need to know three things. First, they need to know *what*. What are the ropes, norms, traditions, and beliefs of the organization? What are the values and ethical commitments of people in this system? What is expected of junior members? What are the hidden traps and landmines? Second, mentees need to know *how*. Good mentors help mentees develop the requisite behaviors, skills, and knowledge needed to succeed. Think of this as equipping your mentees for an arduous journey. What do they need to make it to their destinations? What information should you impart? What skills should you polish? Do they have a current map? Are they prepared to do battle? Do they have an accurate grasp of the terrain that lies ahead? Third, mentees need to know *whom*. Don't forget this. Who are the safe and dangerous actors in the system's cast of characters? Who are their likely allies, foes, or neutral parties? Who are the gatekeepers, the power brokers, the people who hold the most institutional memory? How can mentees begin developing a solid web of supportive relationships? Before sending mentees off, ask yourself if they know the what, how, and whom.

Some mentors are particularly adept at informally transferring knowledge about the workplace through the medium of storytelling. Sharing stories born of experience can help illuminate truths about the organization or profession. Poignant stories become indelible exemplars in the mind of the mentee. The successes and failures of those who have gone before become salient schemas for mentees when they encounter similar circumstances themselves. Some mentors rely on metaphors while others prefer to impart wisdom by sharing personal tribulations and triumphs. Of course, it is essential that mentors only self-disclose for the purpose of teaching. Self-disclosure in the service of self-adulation or selfish catharsis is counterproductive.

Here are three caveats for giving the inside scoop. First, excellent mentors must exercise discretion in their communications. They must transmit crucial insider information without stooping to gossip. It is one thing to instruct mentees about the subtleties of local politics and organizational power; it is quite a different thing to malign colleagues or to be a gossipmonger. Second, good mentors do not demean others in the name of being helpful. They never should resort to sabotaging someone else or nursing a simmering vendetta. These acts do not serve the interests of their mentees. Competent mentors do not create unnecessary rifts between mentees and others in the organization. Third, mentors who have integrity recognize the thin line between the socialization of mentees to the realities of organizational life and cheating the organization in the name of mentoring. They do not disclose classified or similarly designated information, the stuff that is not intended for individuals of their mentee's status or position in the organization. To do so is to behave unethically and unprofessionally.

Recognize the difference between conveying insider wisdom, on one hand, and gossiping, sabotaging, and creating an unfair advantage on the other.

KEY COMPONENTS

- *Socialize mentees by teaching the what, how, and whom of the organization.*
- *Use storytelling as a means of imparting wisdom.*
- *Help develop the mentee's insider understanding of the organization and the profession.*
- *Refuse to undermine colleagues by gossiping under the guise of socializing.*

18

Narrate Growth and Development

With graduate degrees in both management and psychology, Wayne was happy as a lark to land his first job working for a large national consulting firm. The firm specialized in managerial selection and training. Wayne's supervisor, Ron, was an accomplished psychologist and head of training for the firm. Ron had a knack for developing talent, so it was natural for him to see Wayne as an asset to the organization. He also enjoyed interacting with Wayne, and he admired Wayne's ambition and interest in learning the ins and outs of consulting. As their mentorship developed, Ron watched Wayne nervously deliver his first training workshops and tentatively write his initial managerial selection reports. After each such initial foray into consulting work, Ron would take Wayne aside and comment on what he had done well and why this was an important step along the way to mastering consulting skills. As time moved on, Ron discontinued the practice of commenting on each and every report or workshop, but he continued to ob-serve Wayne's performance and made a mental note of his in-creasing competence and confidence. From time to time, Ron would just smile and make supportive statements such as, "You've come a long way, Wayne," or, "You're getting very close to running the workshops on your own; how does that feel?" Long after the mentorship had ended, Wayne recalled that Ron's kind, consistent, and honest narration of his progress was a key ingredient in developing his professional self-confidence.

A mentee needs a mentor to provide narrative and unbiased per-spective on the mentee's movement and change. No one is better situated to narrate the mentee's professional growth and personal development than a mentor. Naïve and overwhelmed, the men-tee can develop tunnel vision—seeing only the hurdles yet to be cleared while overlooking the milestones and progress in the rearview mirror. Seasoned and observant, the mentor can portray the "big-picture" view, helping the mentee to appreciate the distance already covered as well as the terrain ahead.

Having their journeys narrated, especially milestones achieved and skills acquired, gives mentees an occasional opportunity to savor small gains and appreciate good work. To narrate effec-tively, mentors must be intentional, observant, and caring. Men-tors see even modest gains in confidence and performance and describe these to the mentee. They note professional achieve-ments and find avenues for recognizing and even celebrating them. Mentors point out risks taken and label competency where they observe it. Mentors also help place minor setbacks and fail-ures in perspective, detailing the larger picture of development and success. Putting these narrative skills together enables men-tees to gain a realistic appreciation of how far they have come and an objective macro view of their professional progress.

A side benefit of a narrative approach is the strengthening of the mentoring bond. The mentor may be the only person in the mentee's life who takes time to accurately and affirmatively acknowledge growth and change. This mentoring function builds mentee esteem, enhances confidence, and strengthens the mentor–mentee alliance. Consistent and thoughtful narration demonstrates caring and commitment. Mentors who narrate effectively forever hold a special place in the lives of their mentees. They tell the real story of growth, change, and development—a story that will always be etched in the minds of mentees.

In sum, mentors who narrate see in their mentees what the mentees do not see in themselves and use that insight effectively to foster their growth and development.

KEY COMPONENTS

- *Attend carefully to your mentee's small gains and important milestones.*
- *Narrate your observations of development and achievement.*
- *Use these gains to highlight how far your mentee has traveled on the professional journey.*
- *Understand that your affirmative narration will be quite meaningful to your mentee and that it will strengthen the mentorship bond.*

19

Self-Disclose When Appropriate

Jin was petrified when it came to public speaking. Although she was bright and confident in most areas, she had a long-standing public-speaking phobia. Of course, this fear substantially hampered her performance in law school, and as she began a clerkship at a major law firm, she worried that Stephen, her supervising attorney and mentor, would discover this shortcoming and then reject her. Although her legal research and written briefs were outstanding, she avoided Stephen's invitations to participate in depositions and oral briefings. Recognizing Jin's social reticence, Stephen disclosed his own struggle with public speaking earlier in his career. Smiling kindly, he said, "Jin, you remind me of myself in law school. I had a profound fear of speaking and felt like I was going to shake to death every time I had to get up in front of the class. I managed to work through it just by doing it more often, forcing myself to accept speaking engagements, and refusing to get too down on myself. I still get anxious before courtroom appearances, but I deal with it, and people even say I come off pretty well!" Surprised to learn about Stephen's similar struggle, the revelation served as an impetus for Jin. Stephen's revelation not only normalized Jin's anxiety but stoked motivation for her to seek outside coaching and counseling to sharpen her speaking skills.

Authentic self-disclosure has the potential to create more poignant learning, more meaningful change, and a more enduring bond than any other mentor intervention. Sometimes mentors disclose important pieces of their own history, such as critical turning points in their development. Sometimes they disclose their own fears, apprehensions, and struggles. Of course, they share their successes as well. Mentees can be deeply impacted when they hear the less glamorous side of the mentor's personal story. Self-disclosure can be a source of encouragement. Mentees can discover that success does not come without struggle, and their mentor is a living example. Seasoned and self-aware mentors are also comfortable disclosing how the mentorship affects them and what they value most in the mentee. Such disclosure models self-awareness and a willingness to be authentic in the relationship.

Because self-disclosure can enhance intimacy and connection in a relationship, it is not surprising that mentees in many fields rate the willingness to self-disclose as one of the most important qualities in a mentor. When mentors share meaningful experiences or feelings, they show what it means to be authentic, and they model self-exploration. In essence, the thoughtfully revealing mentor opens a window into the self and allows the mentee a glimpse inside. These forays into the life of the mentor must be selective, well timed, and tailored to the mentee's current needs and experiences. When mentees suffer from self-doubt, mentors might share some of their early career struggles. When mentees strain to juggle work and family responsibilities, mentors might relate personal strategies that proved helpful.

When self-disclosure is thoughtful, cautious, and geared to normalizing the mentee's experience, it can be life-changing. Self-disclosure communicates authenticity; it meta-communicates investment in and caring for the mentee while strengthening the bond between the mentor and mentee. But here is a word of caution. Mentors should remain vigilant to any sign that their self-disclosures are leading to codependency or romantic involvement. Authentically disclosing to help a mentee is one thing; embarking on a slippery slope is another.

Self-disclosure is finally an opportunity to demonstrate humility. Genuine and humble mentors disclose their own mistakes and weaknesses; they use their failings to provide vicarious learning experiences for their mentees. Such mentors shun adulation and work against misconceptions born of idealization. Exceptional mentors avoid offering themselves as mastery models (those who have conquered challenges and adversity and who no longer suffer from weakness, fear, or failing). Instead, they are models of coping (those who accept themselves as imperfect yet stand up to life's challenges through the wisdom painfully acquired).

We use the phrase "when appropriate" for good reason. Self-disclosure can be used to great benefit or detriment. The difference is simply this: appropriate self-disclosure is done for the betterment of the mentee, while inappropriate self-disclosure is done for the gratification of the mentor. Because self-gratifying self-disclosure is aimed at enhancing one's stature in the eyes of a mentee, by implication it does not serve the betterment of the mentee.

KEY COMPONENTS

- *Disclose salient personal experiences as a means of teaching, reassuring, and connecting with mentees.*
- *Model humility and self-exploration through appropriate self-disclosure.*
- *Offer mentees a model of coping, not a model of mastery.*
- *Appreciate the power of self-disclosure to heighten intimacy.*
- *Self-disclose only for the benefit of your mentee.*

20

Accept Increasing Friendship and Mutuality

Over a period of three years, Captain Sharp, the commanding officer of a Navy destroyer, had become particularly fond of his primary mentee, Lieutenant Gray. A smart, trustworthy, and ambitious young officer, Lieutenant Gray was also an excellent leader. In Captain Sharp's view, the lieutenant was just the sort of officer the Navy needed to retain and promote. During his tour as CO, Captain Sharp had coached, encouraged, and counseled Lieutenant Gray to balance his roles as husband, father, and naval officer. During the final year of the active mentorship, the two had more frequent informal discussions about a military career, families, and life in general. Lieutenant Gray's family was often invited to dine with the captain and his wife. By the time both officers moved to new commands, they were close friends. In the years that followed, the two stayed in close contact, and Captain Sharp continued to offer guidance, support, and protection throughout the remainder of his career. Captain Sharp later described his mentee as "part junior officer, part son, and part friend."

As a mentee develops and a mentorship seasons, the excellent mentor welcomes and enjoys an increasingly mutual and collegial friendship. Mutuality is the shared respect, trust, and affection that evolve in a reciprocally beneficial mentoring relationship. Although benefits pertain primarily to the mentee during the early phases of the mentorship, later phases of mentorship may be marked by increasing reciprocity. As the mentee requires less direct teaching, training, and support and as the mentee's confidence and independence increase, the mentorship may evolve into a relationship that takes on new dimensions. Research confirms that mentees find this mutual support an essential part of mentoring. The experience of giving and receiving in a safe mentorship prepares mentees to become colleagues to their mentors and to others. When mentors interact with mentees as colleagues, mentees often report feeling deeply and powerfully validated as emerging professionals.

Mutuality requires willingness to give and take on the part of the mentor. Mentors give of themselves in ways we already have described. They authentically self-disclose, demonstrate warmth and honesty, provide evidence of trust in the mentee by offering them participation in high-stakes tasks, and grant access to important personal and organizational information. Mutuality also requires receiving, a willingness to enjoy the mentee, and acknowledging enjoyment of the growing collegial bond. While honoring the personal boundaries needed to maintain a professional relationship, secure mentors allow themselves to see the mentee as a junior colleague. The mentor begins to enjoy the shared interests, emotional connection, and synergistic energy that blossom from investment in the mentorship.

Most mentees like the collegiality that emerges from a maturing mentorship. Not all mentees, however, find this transition comfortable. Some hold personally rigid or culturally hierarchical views of seniors. For these mentees, collegiality with a supervisor is destabilizing and disorienting. Some mentees hold such deep idealization of their mentors that they cannot imagine themselves having anything of substance to offer. Because mentees vary in their attitudes about friendship and mutuality, mentors have to be sensitive to the needs of each mentee. They simply cannot hold the same expectations of collegiality for every mentee or expect mutuality to develop at the same pace in each mentorship.

KEY COMPONENTS
- *Accept and encourage gradually increasing friendship and collegiality with mentees.*
- *Recognize that mentees experience increasing mutuality as professionally validating.*
- *Communicate enjoyment of your increasing friendship with mentees.*
- *Respect mentee preferences for traditional hierarchical relationships; never force mutuality or familiarity.*

21

Teach Faceting

Kendra was in awe of Janice, her mentor of three years in a large university political science department. As a relatively new faculty member, Kendra worked incredibly long hours, and she occasionally became obsessed about getting grants and achieving tenure. At these times, Janice seemed to ask just the right questions about her life outside of the university. She would ask how Kendra's husband was, how often she was getting out to go running (something Janice and Kendra both enjoyed), and about what novel Kendra was reading (her primary pastime outside of work). At times, Janice would actually say something like, "This is just a job Kendra, don't pretend it's your whole life. Do good work, then go home and take care of your marriage, your health, and your life in novels!" Perhaps most convincing, Janice modeled reasonable work hours, wide-ranging hobbies and interests, and a significant commitment to spending time with her family.

The single most time-tested and dependable mantra emanating from the lips of financial advisors the world over is this: Diversify!

Stocks surge and fall, bond markets sag, and real estate follows regional economic whims. The best protection proclaimed is to spread your assets around. As the cliché warns, "Don't put all your eggs in one basket." This advice applies to other areas of life as well. Strangely, far too few mentors offer similar advice to their mentees when it comes to charting a career course.

Various strands of health research indicate that people with a breadth of interests and time investments are better adjusted and more resilient in the face of adversity. When someone's life contains more than a single facet (e.g., work, economic achievement), that person is said to be "multifaceted" and comparatively better off than the singularly focused peer. By developing a range of interests and skills, a person is faceting. The practice of faceting is helpful in one's personal life and in one's work.

Excellent mentors understand that the mentee whose only outlet is work is ill prepared for life and that the mentee who specializes only in one focused area of work is ill prepared for a career. In the event of unanticipated job loss or career-ending illness, the career-only mentee is emotionally destitute and confused. Having invested little in relationships external to work or fulfilling hobbies and recreational involvement, this person lacks the faceting to adjust and move ahead. Similarly, the mentee who rejects opportunities to develop new specialties or practice new approaches becomes occupationally marginalized and vulnerable when organizations change or seek innovation.

So how does the mentor help a mentee become faceted? Two strategies are especially helpful. First, demonstrate an interest in the mentee as a whole person. Ask about the breadth of a mentee's life interests and involvements. Inquire about a mentee's enjoyable activities, hobbies, and important social relationships external to work. Such benign inquiries telegraph a valuing of multifaceted lifestyles. Without violating privacy or becoming intrusive, the mentor shows genuine interest in the mentee as both a person and a junior professional. This mentor behavior says to the mentee, "All of your life commitments, involvements, and interests are important. Remember work is only one slice of who you are."

Second, model faceting in your life. This strategy may be difficult for some mentors. When mentors are workaholics with few interests external to the job, they are ineffective models of faceting. As is true in parenting and teaching, subordinates learn by watching (and only secondarily by listening). The mentor's office may be adorned with pictures of family, and the mentor may inquire about the mentee's own family and yet work 90 hours a week. Alternatively, mentors can model spending time with loved ones, active involvement in hobbies, having close personal friendships, and willingness to experiment with new job tasks and even career opportunities. They should practice what they preach and live by the rule, "Do as I do, not simply as I say." The message they send should be clear: I am more than my current job title, and if my job ended tomorrow, only one facet of my life would change.

KEY COMPONENTS

- *Model a multifaceted lifestyle and refuse to make work your only life commitment.*
- *Inquire as to your mentee's family, leisure, and community connections and reinforce these important life involvements.*
- *Remind mentees that they are more than the sum of their job titles. Do not reinforce exclusive devotion to work.*
- *Encourage mentees to frequently experiment with new specialties and innovations, thereby increasing their career faceting and marketability.*

22

Be a Deliberate Role Model

As a second-year clinical psychology doctoral student, Daniel was flattered when Dr. Mason, a forensic psychologist and senior faculty member, agreed to serve as Daniel's program advisor and mentor. Almost from the outset, Dr. Mason asked Daniel to accompany him to evaluation sessions, court appearances, and professional meetings at which he was an invited speaker. While his peers rarely had individual meetings with their mentors, Daniel was spending several hours each week watching Dr. Mason "do" forensic psychology. As time went on, Daniel was asked to take increasing responsibility for assisting with parts of the evaluations, co-teaching one of Dr. Mason's undergraduate courses, co-presenting papers at meetings, and even assisting with courtroom presentations. Through his frequent firsthand observation of Dr. Mason's work with clients, colleagues, students, and even lay audiences, Daniel developed significant confidence as a junior professional himself. When he completed his doctoral program, Daniel was so comfortable in his role as a professional that colleagues often mistook him for a much more seasoned psychologist. He was prepared to begin a successful forensic practice at once.

Invite mentees to participate with you in various dimensions of your professional life. The best mentors understand that mentees need to watch them perform the activities necessary in a particular field. They appreciate the fact that some complex professional behaviors (e.g., writing a grant, running a meeting, or pitching a proposal to a client) are best learned through observation. In some settings, the code of professional conduct is largely tacit and unspoken—requiring the mentor to quietly teach and demonstrate the art of communication and success in a world largely foreign to the mentee. Mentees are usually eager to accept opportunities to observe and participate with their mentors in the daily minutiae of "being" a professional. In any organization, effective mentors are engaged with their mentees, first teaching and then showing their mentees how to do business. Mentors prompt mentees to watch, practice under the mentor's supervision, and then practice independently.

Excellent mentors intentionally model ethical behavior and professional responsibility. It should be of interest that mentees also learn about ethics vicariously, regardless of the degree to which the mentor is intentional about modeling ethical behavior. Implicit attitudes and explicit behavior communicate more to the mentee than any lecture the mentor might offer. The mentor must be fair, just, and honest in dealings with colleagues, superiors, clients, and the mentee. It is imperative that mentors appreciate the extent to which they are accorded idealized influence in the lives of their mentees. Mentors are initially viewed as trustworthy symbols of success and accomplishment. Regardless of whether their ethics are meritorious, they will become objects of admiration, idealization, emulation, and respect. They can lose the admiration through behavior that is unprofessional or unethical. Fine mentors accept the power accorded role models and use it to intentionally model ethical professionalism.

Interpersonally skilled mentors also stand as high-impact role models, instilling *mental maps* or cognitive *schemas* for effective collegial relationships. That is, as a mentor demonstrates kindness, empathy, emotional intelligence, mutuality, and empowering inspiration, a mentee downloads these behaviors into his or her personal relational maps. Mentoring scholar Belle Rose Ragins (2012) maintains not only that high-quality mentorships are built on strong relational skills but that they simultaneously *generate* the very relational skills a mentee needs to create their own high-quality relationships in the future. Ragins calls these relational *caches*. Keep in mind that your mentees are using your interpersonal behaviors in constructing their own internal maps for how to be good colleagues, professionals, and perhaps one day, excellent mentors.

The professional life of the mentor is played out before the mentee. As a model, the mentor assists the mentee in forging a professional identity. A healthy identity allows for imperfections as well as personal strengths. This means accepting oneself as a professional and a person and refusing to feign omnipotence, omniscience, or perfection. Mentors bear some responsibility for modeling humility, health, and the integration of professional and personal roles. Research indicates that mentees are particularly drawn to mentors who model successfully the management of their professional and personal lives.

KEY COMPONENTS

- *Invite mentees to participate in various aspects of your professional life.*
- *Understand that some professional tasks can only be learned through direct observation.*
- *Accept the idealized influence you hold in relation to your mentees and use it to model excellence and ethical conduct.*
- *Allow mentees to observe at first, but encourage increasing participation and engagement.*
- *Model the interpersonal and relational skills your mentees can use as mental maps or schemas for creating their own collegial relationships with others.*
- *Model humility, health, and integration of personal and professional roles.*

23

Capitalize on Teachable Moments

Edna knew something was wrong, but she couldn't put her finger on it. One of her sharpest mentees, Cheryl, was ordinarily punctual, focused, organized, and way out in front of her peers. But Cheryl's performance recently had begun to slip. She'd been late to work, late with deadlines, and uncharacteristically disheveled and disorganized. Only when Edna kindly but firmly confronted her did Cheryl admit that her elderly mother, suffering severe dementia, had moved in with Cheryl. Rather than share this critical life transition with Edna and others at work, Cheryl had tried to manage everything alone. Finally understanding, Edna closed the door to her office, poured Cheryl a cup of tea, and asked her mentee, "Do you understand how your silence and unwillingness to share your burdens and ask for support threatens to sabotage your career?" Cheryl did not fully understand this until Edna had asked. Together they discussed how Cheryl could become more transparent and authentic when stressful life events occurred. They also discussed the benefits of transparency and the pitfalls of not being transparent. Edna helped Cheryl understand that it is both human and wise to seek and accept support—especially from one's mentor. This is a lesson Cheryl took to heart.

"Life happens," as the popular saying goes. Moreover, "life comes at you fast," as the insurance commercial warns. Events take place in all of our lives that are unexpected, unanticipated, and unplanned. Far from static and predictable, life—including careers—is notoriously fluid, chock-full of abrupt and unexpected challenges. We simply do not know beforehand when they will occur. Some of these unanticipated incidents are pleasant surprises, like getting a big raise. Some are sources of disappointment, like the diagnosis of a close relative or friend with a serious medical condition. In short, no one knows in advance what lies ahead on life's journey.

In a mentorship, unexpected, unanticipated, and unplanned events also occur. Similar to life's journey, neither the mentor nor mentee knows about these occurrences in advance. Some of the occurrences are pleasant, and some are disappointments. Some are simply surprises without strong emotional valence. A mentor and mentee make a serendipitous discovery. Mentees may have a jolting experience that catches them off guard. A mentor comes to realize an undesirable trait in a mentee. These are just samples of the innumerable events that can, without forewarning, force their way into the mentoring relationship.

Although mentors cannot prepare in advance for every unanticipated occurrence, they can anticipate the unanticipated. They can prepare themselves mentally to use these events as "teachable moments." Teachable moments are precious gifts. They are opportunities mentors can seize upon to teach important lessons. Many of the lessons taught during these moments are so powerful and enlightening that no amount of planning in advance could match in impact. As the journey in a mentorship unfolds and teachable moments appear unannounced, mentors should take a pause. At just the right moment, with just the right lesson, using just the right words, they should not pass up these golden opportunities to do high-impact teaching. Their thinking is this: "Stop! Let's capture the real lesson that is now before us. How can this experience inform you for the continued journey that lies ahead?" In summary, a teachable moment is a terrible thing to waste.

KEY COMPONENTS

- *Make yourself comfortable with teachable moments.*
- *Look for opportunities to seize upon teachable moments.*
- *Anticipate the unanticipated.*
- *Be specific about the important lesson in each teachable moment.*
- *Look in retrospect over your experience as a mentor and try to identify teachable moments that passed you by. Use this lesson as a teachable moment for yourself.*

24

Ask Socratic Questions

As one of the few women in the technology division of a major financial firm, Julia felt like an imposter most days. Sure, she had the university degree in IT engineering and just as much experience as the junior men in her division. But she daily received both explicit and implicit messages that as a woman in tech, she was a unicorn. The men around her wondered aloud whether she was competent, and even when she had a big win, she had to prove herself over and over again. Thankfully, her mentor, Denzel, was especially good at deftly helping her to question, challenge, and then reframe her assumptions and self-doubts. When she felt close to quitting and questioned her own competence, he would raise one eyebrow and ask questions such as, "Where did that thought come from? Excuse me, but can you provide one shred of evidence that you are not as competent as or more competent than any of your coworkers? Where is it written that because you're a woman, you have to be perfect? You say that 'everyone' questions your competence, but I don't, so your assumption seems faulty to me, do you agree?" Each time

Julia left Denzel's office, she felt affirmed and emboldened to challenge her own self-doubting beliefs.

Socrates understood the power of a carefully crafted question. The revered Greek philosopher was famous for conducting thoughtful conversations almost exclusively through systematic questioning. Socrates challenged his mentees—the most famous of whom was Plato—to question their own beliefs and assumptions. Using rigorous logic, Socrates helped to clarify even dearly held beliefs, particularly those that sabotaged and stunted his mentees' growth and success.

In the hands of an effective mentor, Socratic questioning involves thoughtful, disciplined, and laser-like inquiries. The mentor's questioning helps mentees to distinguish what they think they know from what they actually know, moving them toward the deeper understanding of what they need to know. Questions are asked for the purpose of revealing the contours of the mentee's dream career, exploring worries and anxieties, and exposing and disputing growth-inhibiting assumptions and beliefs. Socratic questioning is most effective when it is collaborative, gentle, and delivered in a spirit of humble inquiry. Good questioning always enlists the mentee's participation in the discovery process. The beauty and genius of Socratic questioning as a mentoring style is the likelihood that the mentee will experience "ah-ha" moments of insight followed by their own powerful challenge and reframing of faulty assumptions regarding themselves, their potential, and the work environment around them.

A mentor's Socratic questions can take several forms. First, there are *clarifying* questions designed to probe for underlying assumptions and elucidate evidence behind beliefs ("Can you help me understand *why* you say that about yourself? Assuming you could do anything, what would it be? How exactly do you know this? Can you give me a specific example? Aren't you making an assumption here? What do you suppose is causing _____?"). Second, there are *challenging* questions designed to confront erroneous and self-defeating beliefs ("Is there a different way to look at this? Is it really true that *everyone* thinks _____? I wonder if you've ever considered a different possibility . . . does this seem plausible? Where is it written that you can't possibly _____?"). Finally, some Socratic questions focus on *implications and consequences* ("What's the worst that could happen? Imagine if you believed _____ instead of _____, what would that mean for you and how would you feel? If you insist that you can't possibly _____, will that help you achieve it?").

Remember that Socratic questioning is most powerful and meaningful in the context of a trusting and caring relationship. When using questions to challenge and confront assumptions that block a mentee's growth and success, ask him or her in a spirit of humility, collaboration, and genuine respect.

Here is a final caveat. Remember that mentees will sometimes face real resistance, mistreatment, and unfair discrimination in the workplace. Although challenging maladaptive responses to these roadblocks is nearly always helpful, a mentor mustn't ignore the obligation to do more. In the case of Julia and Denzel, Denzel should certainly challenge Julia's self-defeating self-talk, but he should also stand ready and willing to offer sponsorship (element 7), encouragement and support (element 9), protection (element 12), and solid advocacy (element 49).

KEY COMPONENTS

- *Listen for your mentee's explicit and implicit assumptions and beliefs.*
- *Use strategic questions to help mentees clarify their aspirations and assumptions.*
- *Challenge self-defeating beliefs about self, others, and the*

world by carefully questioning a mentee's irrational generalizations and unsupported assumptions.

- *Always use Socratic questioning in a spirit of humility, respect, and care.*

. . .

Traits of Excellent Mentors

MATTERS OF STYLE AND PRESENCE

Having explored the skills of excellent mentors, now let's take a closer look at the person of the mentor. In this section of *The Elements*, we consider the key components of *being* the sort of person to whom mentees are most attracted and find most helpful. These are the characteristics bearing on human presence and interpersonal style. The most important questions are these: What are you like interpersonally? What are your primary relational habits? How does it *feel* for a mentee to be in relationship with you?

Although a wide range of personality features can be found among good mentors (e.g., some are socially introverted while others savor plenty of group interaction; some are compulsively organized while others prefer spontaneity and last-minute planning), there are some intrapersonal qualities and interpersonal habits that predominately contribute to successful mentoring. Mentees, like other human beings, are naturally drawn to and are often helped by mentors who are warm, good listeners, and unconditionally accepting. Mentees also prefer mentors who are trustworthy, sensitive, respectful, and have a good sense of humor.

In this section, we consider the person of the mentor—the interpersonal qualities and characteristics that matter in successful mentoring. Although these particular elements may be more difficult to modify and develop than the previously discussed mentoring skills, all mentors can improve and polish their interpersonal approach. Keep in mind that the important elements in this section have much to do with the real *art* of mentoring.

25

Exude Warmth

As a new junior editor for a medium-sized publishing house, Roger was drawn to Frank—one of the senior book editors. Not only was Frank an accomplished editor and well-liked member of the company, he was also gifted in how he related to people. Coworkers in the office readily took to him. Roger noticed that Frank always made him feel good about himself when the two had a conversation or encounter with each other. It was hard for Roger to put his finger precisely on what happened when they were together, but he was certain about one thing: Frank made him feel special and valued. Actually, Frank possessed a number of favorable qualities. He was kind, genuine, and laughed and smiled easily. He was free with complimentary and supportive comments (e.g., "I can't believe how lucky we are to have you here, Roger. You're a delight to work with"). Frank took the time to inquire about Roger's family and his experience thus far on the job. In Frank's presence, Roger felt like he was ten feet tall.

Like a seed that needs nourishing to germinate and grow, people need the proper ingredients in their environments to flourish. An important ingredient for growth in a mentorship is *emotional warmth*. Mentees across a broad spectrum of arenas rate warmth and caring among the most important mentor traits. Warmth is an attitude of friendliness, approachability, and openness. When mentors radiate warmth, mentees can bask in that emotional sunlight. Warmth translates into respect and being nonjudgmental. Mentees in warm mentorships report feeling accepted, prized, and admired. Mentor warmth charges the mentorship with positive emotional valence. This is because human beings are drawn to warmth, whether it is physical or psychological.

Warmth has verbal and nonverbal components, and you cannot have one without the other. Warmth is communicated verbally through affirming comments (e.g., "You are a delight to supervise"), expressions of concern (e.g., "You seem to be sluggish of late. Are you getting enough rest?"), and statements of appreciation (e.g., "I am so thankful you found the error in the data set"). But to really have a positive impact, these verbal expressions also must be sincere. Sincerity is communicated nonverbally through attentiveness, good eye contact, a soothing tone, kind facial expressions, open and relaxed body posture, and, on some occasions, physical touch when appropriate. Sometimes a simple touch on the arm or pat on the back may say more than a thousand words. Mentors should just be careful not to cross acceptable and cultural boundaries of physical contact.

The opposite of this quality is emotional coolness. Mentors cut of this fabric are destined to seriously limit the value of their relationships with mentees. Under their tutelage, mentees do not feel safe, respected, or cared about. In all likelihood, mentees will not flourish or reach their full potential. Instead, they will use much of their energy staying on guard and trying to figure out where they stand with their mentor rather than putting it to productive use.

Emotional coolness comes from two primary sources. Some mentors simply are detached and insulated. This is their core personality, which represents their defense against pain and trauma. At some level, they just decide that it is not worth the risk of making themselves vulnerable to other people. Cool mentors are difficult to change. Other mentors may have the capacity for warmth but lack the requisite skills for expressing warmth to mentees. A more promising scenario, these mentors simply need to learn and practice the skills of attentiveness, kindness, and emotional availability. By learning from good models and taking the time to practice methods of conveying warmth, most mentors can improve their skills in this area.

KEY COMPONENTS
- *Recognize warmth as a necessary condition for maximal mentee growth and development.*
- *Radiate warmth with an attitude of friendliness, approachability, and kindness.*
- *Consistently offer verbal and nonverbal expressions of sincere interest, thorough acceptance, and genuine positive regard.*

26

Listen Actively

When Linda reflected on her mentorship with Megan, specifically why Megan became such an important figure in her life, she often returned to a recurring experience: sitting in Megan's office and describing a problem or idea while her mentor sat carefully listening to every word. As a senior vice president at a multinational financial institution, Megan's days were crowded to say the least. She still recognized Linda's talents and was committed to guiding her through the ranks of management. Megan demonstrated her commitment through deliberate and focused listening whenever Linda approached her with a question, idea, or concern. On these occasions, Megan would come around her desk, sit in a chair across from Linda, lean forward, and show attentiveness before thoughtfully responding. Linda knew Megan heard every word because her

responses showed a clear grasp of the concern or creative no-
tion. Megan's intentional and skillful listening conveyed a
powerful message: You are very important and well worth this
expenditure of time and energy.

Most people can hear words, but not everyone takes the time to listen. Listening is more than hearing. It is active attention to two levels of communication:

1. the *overt* message—the literal or concrete meaning of spoken words, and
2. the *covert* message—the more subtle or implied meaning.

It is essential that you deliberately work at "hearing" your mentee on both levels. Sometimes, the inconsistency between the overt and covert messages will offer clues to the mentee's real experience.

Mentees rank active listening high among the traits of ideal mentors. Sadly, poor listening is an epidemic in Western culture. Busy mentors can get distracted by emails, text messages, drop-ins by other colleagues, and the near-constant tyranny of the busy schedule. If mentors are not tenacious about creating space for listening, distractions and interruptions may telegraph to a mentee that he or she isn't particularly important to them. And even when they do sit still, close the door, and turn away from social media, mentors may not take the time to truly *attend* to the meanings behind other people's words. In their rush to give a good answer, offer advice, or tell their story, mentors can miss out on opportunities to hear their mentee's real concern or point of view. This inattentiveness communicates that the mentee has nothing worthwhile to say.

Active listening is actually a complex and demanding activity, consisting of several microskills. Here are several that should be especially useful for mentors. Use good nonverbal responses (e.g., nodding, maintaining eye contact, smiling), and make sure these are commensurate with your verbal responses. Use verbal prompts to encourage mentees to express themselves as fully as possible (e.g., "Yes, mm-hmm, tell me more about that"). Do not interrupt. Interruptions are guaranteed to make mentees feel that what they have to say is not important. Ask for clarity about vague comments. This shows mentees that they are being taken seriously. Accurately reflect what mentees communicate. Reflection means to paraphrase or summarize the core themes of the mentee's message; accurate reflection is much harder than you might think! This shows that mentees are being understood.

Here is a final caution about listening. There is evidence that men can struggle more than women with this relational habit. In the book *Athena Rising*, many women indicated that their male mentors would listen to them for only a minute or two in conversations before abruptly jumping in to try and "fix" their problem for them. Apparently, many men are socialized to instantly problem-solve when what mentees primarily need is a listening ear. The chance to be heard by a good listener is all that a mentee may need to get clarity and begin on a path forward.

KEY COMPONENTS
- *Drop other activities when mentees want to talk; give them your undivided attention.*
- *Listen to identify both overt and covert meanings in your mentee's communication.*
- *Ensure congruence between your verbal and nonverbal demeanor; communicate genuine interest and consistent attention.*
- *Reflect (accurately paraphrase) your mentee's primary concerns.*
- *Be diligent about careful listening before offering advice or moving to a solution.*

27

Be Dependable

Charles was a remarkably successful executive director of a large education research institute. Relatively young for someone in his position, he had achieved much through talent, tenacity, and excellent management skills. When Clara took a position as a new project manager with the institute, Charles recognized her as someone with great potential. He began to mentor her and learned that she had interest in an eventual managerial leadership position. The two discussed her ideal career trajectory and the various tasks and positions Clara would need assistance attaining on her way up. During the second year of the mentorship, Charles was inundated with speaking invitations, book offers, and even a request to lead a presidential education initiative. Although he found his schedule becoming absurdly packed, and although he decided he would have to scale back on some of his duties and commitments at work, he was careful to follow through with the biweekly meetings he had scheduled for Clara as well as impromptu conversations about her career. He continued to review drafts of her research carefully and return them expeditiously. As a result, Charles's opportunities and popularity only benefited Clara. She always found him dependable and this significantly bolstered her sense of value and confidence.

When it comes to being a mentor, talk is cheap. It is delightful to begin interacting with a talented and admiring junior. It is harder to follow through with the real work of mentoring. Excellent mentoring demands of the mentor consistency and reliability. It occasionally requires self-sacrifice. Yet, dependability is a cornerstone of mentoring. To say it bluntly: put your time where your mouth is, or do not commit to mentorships.

In a survey of several hundred university graduate students regarding the traits they most wanted in a mentor, one of the top-rated preferences was dependability. The specific item rated highly by students read: "Can always be counted on to follow through when he/she makes a commitment." The message here is loud and clear. Mentees want consistency, dependability, and follow-through—not words but action. Good intentions mean little when they are not backed up by behavior.

So how do mentors demonstrate that they are dependable? First, they stay true to the agreements and commitments made early in the mentorship. Perhaps the simplest yet most often violated corollary of this rule is, attend all scheduled meetings and activities with mentees—don't forget, and don't be late. If you have promised to provide specific mentoring functions or to help the mentee achieve a specific milestone, follow through. Second, mentors should ensure a reasonable turnaround time on commitments to mentees. One of the most frequent complaints made by mentees is that mentors fail to return drafts of reports, proposals, or scholarly work in a timely fashion. If one of your essential avenues for teaching and coaching is reviewing your mentee's work, then do it expeditiously. Otherwise the mentee languishes and professional development slows. Sometimes dependability is communicated simply by speed. Third, mentors need to be emotionally consistent. Nothing destabilizes and diminishes a mentorship faster than an emotionally unpredictable or overreactive mentor. Finally, mentors should avoid the "inspiration only" trap. The mentor who generates creative ideas and collaborative possibilities but fails to follow through is unreliable. The mentee learns not to take this mentor's promises seriously.

There is an unintended consequence of mentor unreliability. When a mentor makes promises and plans with a mentee but fails to follow through, mentees make an interpretation of the disconnect between word and deed. Mentees might conclude that they are a failure, a disappointment, an unimportant entity, or perhaps guilty of causing the mentor to be angry. Certainly, these conclusions are erroneous. Nevertheless, they obviously are corrosive to mentees' self-esteem and confidence. Overall, the unreliable and inconsistent mentor can have a damaging effect on the confidence and identity of mentees. This is unacceptable.

Here is a final paradox for mentors to consider. The most powerful, accomplished, and successful professionals are the very ones who are most vulnerable to being scattered, harried, and unreliable in the mentor role. Successful professionals are in demand. In a malaise of overwhelming demands and overextended schedules, a mentor is tempted to rush, cut corners, and economize when it comes to mentees. Refusing to shortchange a mentee may be one of the most salient traits of an excellent mentor. It takes extraordinary discipline to be a dependable mentor.

KEY COMPONENTS

- *Make following through with commitments to your mentee a top priority.*
- *Provide your mentee with expeditious turnaround and feedback when reviewing his or her work.*
- *Work at emotional stability and consistency. Don't overreact.*
- *Refuse to cut corners when it comes to allocating time to your mentee.*

28

Show Unconditional Regard

When Louise began to mentor Jamal, a college sophomore, she was impressed by his intelligence and promise as a writer. As an English professor with many years of experience, she also recognized Jamal's ambivalence about college, his own ability, and his life and career aspirations. As a mentor, Louise tirelessly encouraged Jamal to write and praised his efforts. She sponsored his short stories for publication and listened carefully to his concerns and hopes. After Jamal briefly dropped out of college before changing his major upon returning, she nevertheless continued to ask him to take "coffee breaks" in the campus grill, praised his talents, and expressed genuine interest in his life and career. Anticipating rejection, Jamal was surprised by his mentor's consistent high regard of him. Although he did not graduate with a major in English, he did begin to write successfully and later attributed much of that success to Louise.

Many achievements in life are based on meeting some predetermined conditions. As the saying goes, "There is no such thing as a free lunch." Homeowners must qualify financially to get a mortgage. Attorneys must pass the bar exam to practice law. And track stars have to run faster than their competitors to win a race.

While mentors have lofty expectations of mentees, there is one area where no conditions should be set: the acceptance of mentees as people and unique individuals. Renowned psychologist Carl Rogers championed this idea of unconditional positive regard—a prime ingredient in the process of positive growth and change. He described this ingredient in such terms as acceptance, nonpossessive caring, and prizing. Mentors demonstrate unconditional regard when they patiently listen, communicate authentic interest, and accept the mentee even when the mentee errs or fails. In fact, a mentor's unconditional regard is most notable when a mentee fails. For not even in failure does the mentee earn the mentor's disregard. Instead, the mentor's message is clear: this mistake or bad outcome does not define who you are. Ideal mentors not only hold positive attitudes about their mentees but express this regard through what they say and how they behave.

Unconditional positive regard has several key components. First, the mentor must communicate an unquestionable commitment to work with the mentee and a freely chosen willingness to do so. More than this, however, the mentor must communicate that the decision to mentor is based on high regard for the mentee's fundamental virtues and extraordinary promise. Commitment is tangibly expressed when the mentor schedules time for the mentee, faithfully keeps appointments, and carefully maintains confidentiality. Of these expressions, scheduling time exclusively for the mentee is particularly imperative. Interactions based only on hurried hallway chats or side conversations during larger meetings convey disregard. Perhaps the greatest damage is done by mentors who are disingenuous. They verbalize their commitments to mentees but disregard them by their actions. Here their actions speak louder than their words.

Second, unconditional regard is communicated through diligent efforts to understand the mentee. Excellent mentors work at understanding their mentee's point of view and communicate this understanding by asking clarifying questions and avoiding the tendency to superimpose themselves on the mentee. Finally, unconditional positive regard requires a nonjudgmental attitude. Effective mentors never jump to a premature interpretation of a mentee's thoughts, feelings, or actions. Instead, the mentor accepts them and works to help the mentee understand how each of these aspects of behavior might influence achievement of his or her personal and professional dreams.

KEY COMPONENTS

- *Regard your mentees as fundamentally and unconditionally good and worthwhile.*
- *Demonstrate consistent acceptance, nonpossessive caring, and even prizing.*
- *Show unconditional positive regard even when mentees fail.*
- *Demonstrate positive regard through commitment of time and resources and efforts at genuine understanding.*
- *Be nonjudgmental and understanding of mentee thoughts, feelings, and actions.*

29

Respect and Safeguard Privacy

A mid-career architect at a large architectural firm, Julian was a magnet for the firm's newest additions. Maybe it was his calm temperament, his sincere interest in helping brand new architects learn the ropes, or his kind disposition. Whatever the reason, Julian was seen by many of the junior architects as a "safe" and supportive mentor. He did more than donate time and effort to teaching his mentees the intricacies of success at a large firm and burnishing their fledgling professional skills. He also made himself available on an emotional plane to provide encouragement, bolster confidence, and lend a listening ear. Over the years, it was not unusual for Julian to find himself the recipient of some very personal disclosures. It was a testament to his genuine compassion that mentees were comfortable disclosing intensely personal fears, marriage woes, serious illnesses, and even conflict with others in the firm. Although he was careful not to posture himself as a professional counselor, Julian was an attentive listener who knew how to express empathy. Of equal or greater importance was his ironclad approach to keeping confidences. Mentee secrets were safe with him, and everyone knew it. When supervisors or colleagues attempted to "go fishing" for private details about one of Julian's mentees, their inquiries were met with a cordial rebuff.

Your mentees have a right to determine the time, location, manner, and extent of their disclosures. In ethical terms, they have a right to privacy. Privacy may be translated as freedom from unsanctioned intrusion. All of us should enjoy the right to keep personal information private. And all of us want to know that the recipients of our personal disclosures will honor our right to privacy.

Mentors, then, are obligated to respect mentee privacy. There are several ways to communicate this respect. First, do not coerce those you mentor into disclosures of personal information. Remember that coercion can be direct or indirect, overt or covert. Show deference to each mentee's right to self-determination and privacy. As a mentor, your legitimate interest in your mentee can subtly cross over into unwanted intrusion. So be careful. You just might find it a challenge to bridle your curiosity. You show your respect by allowing your mentees to set the pace and determine what is important for them to self-disclose. At all costs, avoid intrusive or highly personal questions—those unrelated to a mentee's professional development—such as questions about romantic relationships or personal finances.

Second, be sensitive to personal preferences. Mentees vary considerably on the topics they are willing to share. Some mentees are more private than others, and mentors need to appreciate this variation. After all, everyone has a unique combination of family experience, cultural background, gender, and personality characteristics, causing them to occupy different locations on the continuum of disclosure and privacy. The job of the mentor is to ascertain the expectations of each mentee and respond genuinely to each one's self-disclosures.

Third, when discussing mentees with others or writing about them (e.g., responding to verbal inquiries, writing letters of recommendation), focus exclusively on the salient elements of their professionalism and performance. Avoid sharing information that is irrelevant to work. For instance, mentors should offer their assessment of a mentee's fitness for a promotion or new job in the organization. As long as the assessment is fair and unbiased, the provision of the information is warranted. However, sharing information that is irrelevant to job performance is inappropriate. Discussing a mentee's religion, relationship history, sexual orientation, or private career aspirations is not warranted.

In addition to respecting the right to privacy, excellent mentors also protect information a mentee entrusts to the mentor in confidence. Honoring confidentiality is the deliberate protection of personal or private information disclosed by a mentee in the context of a mentorship. The disclosure may be an intentional effort to provide the mentor with a clearer understanding of the mentee or merely a reflection of intimacy and trust in the mentor–mentee bond. In either case, the wise mentor understands that confidentiality is core to any effective relationship. Counselor–counselee, attorney–client, doctor–patient, and mentor–mentee are all relationship forms that hinge on this assumption: what is disclosed in the relationship stays in the relationship. Although confidentiality is primarily an ethical obligation, not a legal one, in the context of mentorship, violating confidentiality, like intruding on privacy, always increases the probability of relational damage.

Should mentors ever violate a mentee's confidentiality? Although the general rule is to protect confidentiality, there are special circumstances in which the disclosure of confidential information is not only appropriate but required—even without the mentee's consent. Prominent examples are when a mentee makes a suicide threat, threatens to harm someone else, is caught in embezzlement, or demonstrates impairment that prevents them from performing their responsibilities at work. The decision to disclose confidential information is undoubtedly tied to the specific profession, work setting, and a host of legal considerations. For instance, in some professions (e.g., aviation, police work, law, military), a mentor may be legally obligated to disclose criminal behavior or mental instability on the part of a mentee. At the same time, a college advisor may be legally obligated by the Family Education Rights and Privacy Act (1974) to protect all records of his or her advising and mentoring work with a mentee.

The important question is this: do mentees understand the limits to confidentiality in their mentoring relationship? Wise mentors should discuss the limits of confidentiality early in their mentorships—particularly in those professions that may require mentor disclosure of confidential information in specific circumstances—to make certain there is mutual understanding about the factors that might trigger a disclosure. In the end, a mentor who respects privacy and protects confidentiality will garner respect in return. And mentees who respect their mentors benefit from the mentoring relationship.

KEY COMPONENTS

- *Avoid unnecessary intrusions into the personal world of your mentees.*
- *Protect any information or disclosure shared by a mentee in confidence.*
- *Discuss any limits on confidentiality early in the mentorship.*
- *Exclude private information about a mentee from any communication to others.*

30

Tolerate Idealization

Fresh from the Naval Academy and a newly minted ensign, Brett stood in awe of his first department head, Commander Creighton. Not only was the commander a veteran of naval combat, the recipient of numerous awards, and a shoo-in for eventual promotion to admiral, he was also an inspiring leader. He was poised, articulate, interpersonally savvy, and intellectually sharp. In addition, Commander Creighton showed interest in Brett and began to offer advice and challenge. Although Brett was initially nervous, befuddled, and practically worshipped his boss, Commander Creighton remained kind, humble, and tolerant. He understood that Brett's reverence was a necessary early step in their mentorship. He further understood that attempting to pop Brett's bubble by airing his human weaknesses and imperfections was unlikely to assist Brett's development. Over time, in the context of a strong mentorship, Brett's idealism was tempered by a more reality-based picture of his mentor. Still, he deeply admired many of the commander's techniques and traits and adopted many of these in his own leadership style. Later, when the two had gone their separate ways, an astute observer would note that although Brett manifested many of Commander Creighton's characteristics, he expressed these uniquely, in a professional style that had become his own.

After ducklings hatch, they enter a short but critical period of development. They identify a parent and proceed to mimic and model each of this parent's behaviors. They follow this parent everywhere and never let him or her out of sight. This imprinting process is instinctual and crucial for survival. Imprinting also occurs in humans. Children idealize their parents. The good father smiles but understands not to chasten the fawning son who insists upon accompanying him everywhere, mimicking his behaviors and expressions, and generally getting underfoot. Something tells the father that this is essential. The wisest parents enjoy this stage while it lasts.

Some mentees may need to idealize their mentors early in the relationship. Initially it can be the gateway to healthy *identification*, but idealization poses some significant problems if mentees get stuck there. After identification, mentees can move to *individuation* as a mature and separate professional. For this process to unfold, mentors must learn to gracefully tolerate mentee idealization.

Idealization is a normal developmental process. We all go through it several times during our lives. Idealization involves finding characteristics we do not possess but observe in others—characteristics we admire and wish to develop or discover. Idealization is the necessary process by which we locate and identify those things we want to become. Idealization fosters growth and empowers us. As young children, we typically idealize parents or important caregivers. Literal and figurative giants of strength, power, and virtue, parents exhibit much for the young person to idealize. Later, as adolescents and young adults, we idealize others with whom we relate. These idealized others serve as templates for our ambition. A competent and accomplished mentor is the perfect person to fit the bill. Mentees need to admire and idealize the mentor. They need to look upon the mentor's traits, skills, and polished mannerisms through rose-colored glasses. Like the ducklings, they need that critical period of waddling behind their mentor. Mentors should not be put off by this behavior. If they do their jobs right, it won't last forever.

Although idealization helps to motivate a mentee to enter a mentorship, it subsides and is ideally replaced by something else—identification. Less idealistic and biased, identification reflects the degree to which the mentee wants to be like the mentor. It is an important process whereby aspects of the idealized are internalized and become the mentee's own. This is a crucial developmental task for the mentee. In effect, the mentee uses initial idealization to identify desirable characteristics and form a personal sense of self. What begins as idealized excitement and awe at the outset of a mentorship can evolve into internalized goals and ambitions. The mentee takes what he or she needs from the mentor to craft a professional identity and eventually individuate.

Here is the crucial piece for mentors: gracefully recognize and tolerate idealization—it is a core feature of good mentoring, and the mentee needs the mentor to allow it to occur. You may be uncomfortable with adulation, but keep in mind that this really is not about you. It is about professional neophytes working to clarify who they will become. Be honored yet humble when idealized. Your mentee needs permission to "imprint": to waddle along proudly in your shadow for a period of time. Later, idealization will be less urgent and more realistic—paving the way for healthy identification of those traits the mentee most wishes to emulate. If tolerated well, idealization will allow your mentee to move from follower to colleague. That is the goal.

KEY COMPONENTS
- *Accept the probability that your mentee needs to initially see you through idealized lenses.*
- *Tolerate idealization and adulation with grace and humility.*
- *Remember that idealization turns to identification and that identification is crucial for professional identity development.*
- *As your mentee matures, he or she can see you in a more balanced and realistic way.*

31

Embrace Humor

A fifteen-year veteran of Congressman Smith's staff and an excellent and energetic aide, Joe immediately appealed to Bonnie as a potential mentor. Not only was Joe quick to help Bonnie learn the ropes around the office, he was kind, supportive, and genuinely interested in helping Bonnie succeed. Joe also had a good sense of humor that he frequently used to help Bonnie take the edge off of her tendency to exaggerate her mistakes and punish herself for perceived shortcomings. When Bonnie began to do so, Joe would often lower his voice conspiratorially, frown, and say something like, "Yes Bonnie, your mistake will probably cost the congressman his career. Not only that, it may cause a downturn in the economy, lead to a new world war, and send the globe into chaos. Thanks a lot, Bonnie." Bonnie would not only laugh but was quickly able to recognize her fruitless tendency toward self-criticism.

Nothing can take the place of a good laugh. Laughter is a soothing balm—medicine to the soul. Perhaps this is why mentees rank humor as one of the five top traits of ideal mentors. A mentor with good humor often is perceived as fully human, approachable, and fun to be around. In the anxiety-ridden world of neophyte mentees, humor serves several important functions: it normalizes the experiences of mentees, minimizes their fears, and reminds them that few things in life are really catastrophic.

One of the best uses of humor in a mentorship is in helping mentees not take themselves too seriously. How often have we seen mentees place ridiculous demands on themselves (e.g., "I *must* make a brilliant presentation at the staff meeting," or, "If I don't get this report done precisely when I promised, it will prove I'm an idiot")? These types of demands and self-judgments obviously are both unreasonable and self-defeating. For many people in such a state of irrationality, a humorous challenge with paradoxical intention might be just the trick: "You're right, it would be absolutely awful if you didn't speak perfectly at the meeting. In fact, it's the worst thing I can imagine. Both of us would probably be finished with our careers and end up on the streets."

Humor can also diminish anxiety about the realities of life and career. Life is hard and so is work. The possibility of occasional failure in either is real. Therefore, mentees cannot afford to take them lightly. But they cannot take themselves so seriously that work and play are artificially divorced. The good mentor helps his or her mentee learn how to moderate serious business with humor, how to mix career with play. Sometimes the best thing mentors can do is to use humor and make light of themselves. Everyone has "blown it" and stumbled along the way. When mentors can be lighthearted about some of their mistakes (both historical and present), they indirectly encourage their mentees. Research indicates that mentees are drawn to "down-to-earth" mentors, those who can fall flat and get up laughing. But remember, humor can have a downside.

Used inappropriately, humor can be counterproductive, even harmful. This is especially true when mentors use humor to belittle a mentee or trivialize important matters. When humor gratifies a mentor without edifying the mentee, something is wrong. Also, some mentees have little capacity for humor and respond poorly to humorous interventions even when they are well intended and nicely delivered. Excellent mentors read mentees accurately and use humor only when mentees are receptive.

KEY COMPONENTS

- *Laugh at yourself often as a means of modeling humility and perspective.*

- *Use humor to help mentees take themselves less seriously.*
- *Teach mentees to mix work and laughter.*
- *Avoid using humor to belittle mentees or trivialize matters important to them.*

32

Gently Confront Perfectionism

As a new brokerage trainee, Joel often felt like an "imposter." He was relieved when Tricia, a more experienced broker, began offering him advice, coaching, and reassurance. Tricia became concerned, however, when she noticed Joel frequently pulling "all-nighters" to complete projects, refusing to bring reports to closure until he believed they were error free, and appearing full of shame and humiliation whenever an error or discrepancy was noted in something he wrote or reported. Tricia began to gently but consistently confront Joel's perfectionistic behavior by saying things like, "Joel, I know you're trying to do good work here, and you are. But perfection is unattainable, so I'm asking you to stop striving for that. You look tired and unhappy. Does your demanding perfection improve your work or your mood?" Over time, she also shared some of her own strategies for developing reasonable goals and helped Joel to make light of minor errors and imperfections.

No one is perfect—not even the brightest and the best. As the old saying goes, "To err is human." Therefore, mentors always should encourage excellence, but not even for a moment should they send the wrong message that a mentee must be perfect. Much of what disturbs mentees involves their unrealistic and perfectionistic attitudes about life, work, and themselves. Too many high-achieving mentees erroneously equate excellence with perfection. This is a profound mistake. Striving for excellence can be motivating and stimulating; demanding perfection is toxic. In truth, the notion of "good perfectionism" is an oxymoron.

Research on perfectionism as a personality syndrome reveals that it consists of two core elements. First, perfectionists set impossibly high—and clearly unattainable—standards for their own performance. Second, perfectionists are relentless in severely criticizing themselves for failing to achieve those performance hurdles.

Perfectionism often stems from early life experiences. Perfectionistic mentees often hail from environments that promulgate a "zero-defect" attitude about performance. In adulthood, perceived shortcomings are cause for severe self-recrimination, and mentees will expect similar intolerance and rejection from mentors. The net effect of perfectionism is diminished enjoyment of work and life. Ultimately, perfectionists are afraid of failure, worried about even the possibility of committing a mistake. Many might be described as "working scared." As psychologist Thomas Lorch says, "A perfectionist is motivated by a fear of failure and a sense of duty rather than enthusiasm for the creative process."

Competent mentors communicate a vision of the mentee as human. Sure, mentees are gifted and talented, but mentors also see their shortcomings and accept them as imperfect. And in the words of psychiatrist David Burns, mentors understand that perfectionism is a "script for self-defeat." For these reasons, the excellent mentor is cautious about communicating, whether intentionally or not, expectations for perfect performance. They discern the difference between high expectation and inhuman demand. Although some perfectionistic communication is overt (e.g., "Now do it again, and this time get it perfect"), the more common and destructive messages to mentees are insidious and subtle. For example, a derisive shake of the head or rolling of the eyes may tell mentees much more about your requirements of them than all of your verbal reassurances combined.

So how can a mentor help mentees avoid perfectionistic thinking and behavior? Here are some tried and true strategies for helping your mentee confront, or better yet, prevent perfectionism:

1. *Check your own perfectionistic tendencies at the door.* If you sometimes struggle with unreasonable standards and self-criticism, be extra cautious about subtly endorsing mentee perfectionism.

2. *Do not make your approval or support contingent on error-free performance.* Focus validation and affirmation on your mentee, not his or her performance. Use mentee errors and mistakes to cultivate a sense of curious inquiry about what went wrong and how to make corrections.

3. *Employ well-timed disclosures about your own missteps.* Reveal how you have learned from professional errors and how each was an opportunity for growth.

4. *Firmly, kindly, and humorously confront perfectionistic thinking.* Ask Socratic questions that help reveal perfectionistic beliefs ("I'm confused why you're insisting that you be perfect. Like the rest of us, you seem to be human, and, of course, we know that to err is human. Can you help me understand that?"). Or try some lighthearted humor ("I can't help but notice that you constantly say you '*should* have' or '*shouldn't* have' . . . I suspect all that *shoulding* on yourself isn't getting you anywhere"). Finally, use humorous paradox to reveal a mentee's catastrophic thinking about the possibility of imperfection ("Yes, I'm certain you are right. If there is even one typo in that document you are creating, I'll

bet both of us will be fired on the spot, end up home-
less, and never find work again").

5. *Deliberately model imperfection and human limitations.*
   Remember that saying "I don't know, let's find out together" can give your mentees permission not to have
   all the answers.

KEY COMPONENTS

- *Celebrate excellence without demanding perfection.*
- *Help mentees discern the dysfunctional nature of perfection-*
  istic attitudes and beliefs.
- *Avoid subtle or nonverbal as well as overt messages that*
  perfection is required.
- *Serve as an intentional and transparent model of imperfect*
  excellence.
- *Use Socratic questions and thoughtful humor to challenge*
  perfectionism.

33

Attend to Interpersonal Cues

Chris often marveled at his mentor's "way with people." A
professor in Chris's MBA program, Dom had become Chris's
mentor when they realized that they both shared several interests
and Chris expressed a desire to earn a PhD. Dom was one of the
few people who could really "read" Chris's emotions and worries
before Chris said a word. Dom was a master at accurately iden-
tifying both his own feelings ("Chris, I have to tell you, not get-
ting that grant has left me feeling depressed today") and those of
others ("Chris, you look anxious. Should we talk about it?"). It
seemed to Chris that Dom was able to tailor his demeanor and
approach to "fit" Chris's mood and his specific mentoring needs.

Given a choice, most mentees would prefer a mentor who has keen interpersonal competence over one who has a powerful intellect. In other words, exceptional mentoring is about much more than IQ. Psychologist and author Daniel Goleman uses the phrase *emotional intelligence* to convey the importance of relating competently to others. In addition to their warmth, active listening, and empathy, interpersonally competent mentors "read" relational cues and use their reading to maximize the health and productivity of the relationship. These mentors are kind, competent, and fun to be around. They exude competence and confidence in the emotional realm. For these reasons, they are sought out by mentees for guidance and advice.

Several distinct skills characterize emotionally intelligent mentors. First, they are self-aware. They understand their own psychological dynamics—their moods, emotions, and drives—and they understand how these affect other people. Second, they have self-control. They allow themselves to experience the full range of human emotions, but when disappointment sets in, they do not become depressively dependent, and when frustrated, they do not become volcanically enraged. Instead, they can express their disappointment in ways that are healthy and constructive. Third, they tune in to the emotional makeup of other people. They read verbal and nonverbal cues. Because of this skill, they often are effective as cross-cultural mentors. Fourth, they are proficient in building social networks. Not only can they find common ground and build rapport with mentees, they do so with colleagues and superiors as well. As a result of their friendliness and interpersonal savvy, they have the knack for positively impacting people and constructing alliances that ultimately benefit both themselves and their mentees (e.g., mentees have access to a broader range of connections and associates).

Emotional intelligence may be one of the most underrated and unexplored characteristics of great mentors. To prove the point, observe traffic flow patterns of mentoring in any organization. Typically, you will see mentees flocking to prospective mentors with proven skills on the emotional/interpersonal plane. Experience shows and research supports the principle that mentees are drawn to emotionally skilled mentors. To conclude, it's great for mentors to have a high IQ but greater for them to have high emotional intelligence.

KEY COMPONENTS

- *Pay attention to your own emotional life and demonstrate emotional self-awareness.*
- *Model a range of appropriate human emotions without expressing emotion impulsively or destructively.*
- *Work to accurately understand the emotional states of mentees.*
- *Use kindness, interpersonal savvy, and emotional awareness to build professional relationships. These will benefit your mentees.*

34
Be Trustworthy

Art's integrity was one of the things Aaron most respected about his mentor. Art was always honest, dependable, and known around the engineering firm as a reliable and "upfront" guy. For this reason, Aaron felt nervous but not overwhelmed when he admitted his painkiller addiction to Art. Although accepting, kind, and respectful, Art told Aaron in clear terms that he would be required to enter treatment, that Art would keep Aaron's disclosure private (only those in management with a legitimate need to know would be involved), and that while he would support Aaron fervently, he would also recommend termination if Aaron's addiction interfered with his perfor-

mance over time or if he continued to use substances and placed the company or others at risk. Aaron's trust in Art was reaffirmed by this experience.

Ideal mentors are trustworthy. They mean what they say and say what they mean, creating a safe and reliable haven for mentees. Trust might be described as mentees' perception that mentors will not mislead or hurt them. Because of a mentor's status and reputation, a certain amount of trust is automatically accorded the mentor. As the mentorship matures, trust is earned. Mentors must demonstrate through unwavering consistency that they are worthy of the mentee's continued trust.

Mentors garner trustworthiness through several avenues. One avenue is through their integrity or fidelity. Fidelity involves honesty and promise-keeping in relation to others. These qualities also extend to broader organizations. Not only do trustworthy mentors adhere to codes of legal and ethical conduct, they are fundamentally committed to internalized moral principles, always striving to be persons of virtue and character. Because it is impossible for mentors to anticipate every moral or ethical quandary they will encounter, they are faithful to undergirding moral principles, such as care and justice, and always place the welfare of those who depend upon them (mentees) before their own needs and interests. It is of note that mentors garner trust when they honestly acknowledge and confront mentees for their mistakes or bad behavior. Apparently, this conveys to mentees that their mentor will prove to be faithful and reliable whether or not the situation is comfortable. Finally, mentors express fidelity by monitoring themselves and their own mentoring behavior. Apparently, mentors who check themselves can be trusted to create healthy and respectful interactions with their mentees.

Mentors also generate trust through genuineness. Their words, actions, and feelings are consistent and transparent. Genuine mentors adhere to the same time-honored principles and values regardless of the situation or who is observing them. What you see with these mentors is what you get. They do not play on their one-up position, and from the highest-level to the lowest-level person in the organization, they always show respect.

To find out what a mentor is really made of, mentees sometimes test their mentors. Under examination is their trustworthiness. Testing comes in a variety of forms, but each is an imperative for mentors to get a passing grade. One mentee may confide in the mentor a deeply held secret or private disclosure. This mentee really wants to know if the mentor can safeguard privacy. Another mentee may request of the mentor additional time or assistance. This mentee really wants to know if he or she is as important as the mentor claims. At times, a mentee will disclose a failure or shortcoming. This mentee wants to see if the mentor is unconditionally accepting. And still another mentee may deliver unsatisfactory work. This mentee may be testing the mentor's resolve to hold to his or her standards of performance.

KEY COMPONENTS

- *Demonstrate trustworthiness with consistency, reliability, and integrity.*
- *Keep promises to mentees.*
- *Adhere to professional and organizational codes.*
- *Honestly confront problems, mistakes, and shortcomings.*
- *Ensure congruence in word and deed.*
- *Maintain confidence and protect mentee disclosures.*

35

Respect Values

As vice president for operations, Connie was in a powerful position to develop new managers aspiring to make the climb. She became impressed with Brinnell, a junior manager in her division. Brinnell was bright, energetic, and also impressed with Connie. Before long, Connie had taken an interest in Brinnell. The two of them began working closely on some projects. They enjoyed frequent discussions designed to prepare Brinnell for success and advancement. Soon, however, Connie discovered that Brinnell was quite conservative in her political views and family values. Connie considered herself a liberal, a feminist, and a lifelong Democrat. For a time, she struggled to accept that her new mentee's politics and values were so different from her own. Aware of the value difference between them, Connie acknowledged this to Brinnell and even made light of how a Democrat and Republican could ever work together. She then worked at supporting Brinnell without coercing her to adopt more liberal views—recognizing and accepting that Brinnell's beliefs and lifestyle commitments may diverge in important ways from her own.

Shared values undergird strong relationships. We are drawn to people who share our sense of right and wrong, our sense of justice, and our beliefs about the things we deem important in life. Conversely, we are less attracted to people who have dissimilar values. Not surprisingly, great mentor–mentee pairs often value similar ideas and commitments. Even when values are discordant at the outset of mentoring, we find that values shift over time so that mentor and mentee values become more congruent. Research confirms that the better the value match within a mentoring pair, the better the mentoring outcomes and the closer the mentoring bond.

When mentee values (ethical/moral, societal, religious) shift to more closely approximate those of the mentor, we call this values *conversion* or values *assimilation*. It seems to be an inevitable outcome whenever an impressionable mentee in any field works closely with an admired and successful mentor. Mentees adopt the behaviors, professional practices, and, over time, the values of an influential mentor. Although experts may caution mentors to be "value neutral" in dealings with mentees, we assert that this is an improbable stance. Mentees inevitably will become aware of the mentor's values on important issues no matter how much the mentor strives for neutrality. Therefore, "neutrality" is neither realistic nor desirable. It is preferable that mentees see the mentor's value positions without feeling coerced to adopt them. This requires mentors to be constantly vigilant regarding their own needs for agreement from subordinates and conscious of their influential position with mentees.

How do mentors create conflict over values with mentees? First, mentors can attempt to interfere with the freedom of mentees to choose their own values. Along these lines, they may offer conditional approval, protection, or continuation of mentoring contingent upon the mentee adopting the mentor's values. Second, through overt coercion, mentors can intentionally impose their own values on mentees (e.g., "Adopt my beliefs and perspectives or else!"). Third, mentors can become judgmental or moralistic. They may condemn the character of the mentee for failing to adopt or agree with their values. Fourth, mentors can be propagandizing. They may handle value issues in a biased manner. This action communicates to mentees that only certain options regarding values are healthy or valid in the eyes of the mentor. Finally, mentors can use subtle coercion. They may use selective reinforcement (nodding, smiling, or verbally affirming only when the mentee voices value perspectives that match the mentor's own). Such coercion may occur without the mentor being consciously aware.

KEY COMPONENTS
- *Understand that the "pressure" is on your mentee to shift values in the direction of your own.*
- *Do not pretend to be value "neutral." Acknowledge your core beliefs and values.*
- *Respect your mentee's values and work to avoid direct values conversion through coercion or propagandizing.*
- *Acknowledge and discuss value differences when appropriate.*

36
Do Not Stoop to Jealousy

As Larry's mentorship with Yolanda progressed, he became increasingly aware of her unusual talent as a researcher and writer. A PhD candidate in biology, Yolanda began publishing single-authored articles in major journals. Initially threatened by his mentee's success, Larry quickly realized the need to put aside his own feelings of competitiveness and even a touch of jealousy and unconditionally and actively support Yolanda. To that end he praised her successes and urged her on. He even encouraged the development of a secondary mentorship with an African American woman who was a scholar in another graduate department on campus. He did so because Yolanda had expressed feelings of racial alienation in the all-white biology department.

Some circumstances remind mentors of their limitations. One important reminder is when mentees show talents and gifts that surpass their mentors. Another important reminder is when their mentees benefit from other mentorships. Instead of becoming jealous, mentors should celebrate their mentees' gifts and opportunities. They should encourage mentees to develop mentoring constellations or networks. Such constellations typically consist of one primary mentorship as well as secondary mentorships.

Secondary mentorships are typically shorter in duration, characterized by less emotional bonding than a primary mentorship, and focused on specific functions, such as learning the ropes in a new specialty area. Mentees sometimes seek secondary mentors to fulfill needs that cannot be met in the primary mentorship. Secondary mentors often have specialized knowledge or expertise that the primary mentor does not have. And the secondary mentoring could be vital to the mentee's development. Additionally, mentees may seek out someone of their race, gender, or religious faith who can identify with their unique cultural and emotional challenges. Mentees sometimes benefit both from peer mentorships where there is greater mutuality, emotional support, and friendship, and from relationships with senior personnel in other departments or professionals in other organizations.

It is never in the best interest of anyone for mentors to become jealous, possessive, or territorial. If they become jealous, mentors send a message to mentees that goes something like this: "This is a safe and helpful relationship only as long as you don't become too successful or autonomous." This reaction places mentees in a double bind and compromises their potential for maximal development. Mentees of jealous mentors may sabotage or cover up evidence of their own growth and success. These mentees are forced to make a painful choice: downplaying themselves to protect the mentor's ego or fully actualizing themselves at the expense of garnering the mentor's support. Neither choice is desirable.

Jealousy, paradoxically, is detrimental to mentors themselves. Jealous mentors force healthy mentees to leave the relationship or produce below their capabilities. They also create a reputation that will deter other potential mentees from entering a mentorship with them. In general, the potential returns and benefits to the mentor are lost.

To counter this reaction, mentors should explore the causes of their jealousy, work diligently to put their feelings in check, and place the mentee's welfare above their own needs for affection, friendship, and adulation. In human relationships, jealousy signals a perceived threat. Jealous reactions are self-protective; they are designed to shield oneself from the threat of ego wounding. Jealous mentors find their egos endangered by mentees who achieve beyond their own capacity or who no longer depend on them as they did earlier in the relationship. Mentors should use their jealousy to serve as a red flag that they have lost sight of their primary purpose. Finally, they should use their jealousy to determine if their reaction reflects an unhealthy emotional involvement with the mentee.

KEY COMPONENTS
- *Remember that jealousy undermines mentoring and nearly always signals your own fear and insecurity.*
- *Use jealous feelings to reorient to the purpose of mentoring: the mentee's development.*
- *Encourage mentee autonomy and celebrate mentee success.*
- *Encourage secondary mentorships to maximize mentee growth.*

. . .

Arranging the Mentoring Relationship

MATTERS OF BEGINNING

One of our prime motivations for writing *The Elements* is to help our readers avoid becoming incidental mentors—professionals who stumble into the role without forethought or deliberate consideration. Instead, we encourage our readers to become *intentional mentors*—professionals who deliberately initiate relationships with promising junior members of the profession and skillfully manage the development and course of mentorships.

In this section of *The Elements*, we discuss the all-important process of intentional and thoughtful arrangement of mentorships. It should be obvious that a good mentorship begins with a good match between mentor and mentee. CEOs, members of graduate school faculties, and marriage partners all over the world know that finding the right "match" is everything. Therefore, to initiate a successful mentorship, the matching of mentees with mentors should not be approached lightly. Since mentors often have a choice in their selection of mentees, they tend to have more success when they choose wisely and have a reasonable sense of a good match. In addition, whenever possible, mentors should structure new mentorships to ensure maximal benefits to mentees and add to the overall success of the relationship. In some organizations, training in mentoring and formal mentoring programs are available. But this is not often the case, especially in smaller organizations, necessitating mentorships that evolve spontaneously and organically over time.

Whether a mentorship begins formally or informally, what occurs in the earliest stages is critical. In particular, mentors must clarify their expectations and the relational boundaries to be maintained. Mentees tend to appreciate this clarification. Furthermore, mentors may use the outset of a mentorship to open a conversation of cultural differences between themselves and a mentee. The intent of the conversation is to ascertain how their differences might impact the relationship. These early steps taken by mentors have the potential of setting the mentorship on a productive course.

Excellent mentors plan for development, change, and, perhaps paradoxically, even ending a mentorship at the outset. But mentors need to have a long-term perspective. The perspective starts at the beginning of the relationship. From the outset, mentors also shoulder the responsibility for evaluation. They evaluate on multiple levels: assessing their own competence as a mentor, assessing the growth and development of their mentees, and periodically evaluating the relationship to determine if it is productive and helpful. By no means should they place that burden of evaluation on the shoulders of mentees. Finally, mentors must plan for the mentees' increasing independence and, at some point, redefining or ending the mentorship.

37

Carefully Consider the "Match"

A senior researcher at the National Institute of Health, Dr. Kalb was known as a markedly influential scientist and a successful mentor to several generations of junior researchers in her field. Many of her mentees had gone on to attain eminence in the sciences. When asked about the "secret" to her success as a mentor, Dr. Kalb would smile and say, "Simple. I only mentor a few scientists at a time, and usually only those who possess great raw talent and tenacity. They are hardworking and intellectually curious researchers who would probably be very successful without my help. So, you might say I cheat and only mentor the great ones! It's really more than that though; I get to know all the new researchers but only mentor those I connect with, those who share my specific interests, and those who don't mind working as many long hours as I do."

Oil and water do not mix. Neither do some mentors and some prospective mentees. It is a matter of chemistry. To increase the chances that your mentorships will flourish, spend time getting to know prospective mentees and try to figure out if you are compatible. A substantial body of research finds that mentors and mentees who are well-matched on important personal and professional dimensions form stronger, more enduring, and more beneficial relationships. Good matching depends heavily on the context of mentoring and mentoring tasks. But personality traits (e.g., sense of humor, warmth, humility, extroversion), social skills, communication style, writing ability, personal values (e.g., importance of work-life balance, religious commitment), short- and long-term career goals, and desired career trajectory also matter in the match.

A salient cluster of matching variables between mentor and mentee has been identified. These include work ethic, need for achievement, drive, and grit. Mentors should ask themselves a couple of questions. To what extent does a prospective mentee share my preference for structure, productivity, and rapid turnaround? Is mutual sharing and friendship more important? How does a mentee fit with the relative emphasis I place on task and relationship orientations? Mentorships that are poorly matched in these areas are sometimes doomed to fail. For instance, the mentor will be frustrated by the mentee's lack of ambition, or the mentee may find the mentor too complacent or relaxed.

According to studies on mentoring outcome, the more mentors and mentees consider themselves to be similar, the greater the *perceived benefits* of the mentorship. For obvious reasons, this finding is consistent with research on marriage. Although opposites occasionally attract, compatibility better predicts positive relationship outcomes. Some of the perceived benefits of well-matched mentorships are particularly worth noting. Mentees from well-matched mentorships report receiving more social *and* career opportunities. Further, well-matched mentors and mentees are both more satisfied with and committed to the relationship.

Intentional consideration of a match assumes first an informal period of mentoring. Here the mentor and mentee have an opportunity to get to know each other due to their close working proximity. These arrangements often develop because the two parties work together without the pressure of a commitment to a formal relationship. Then both parties are free to be themselves. It should be of interest to note that although formally assigned mentorships do increase the rate of mentoring in an organization, they suffer the risk of being more superficial and less effective than informally evolving mentorships. And it all relates to chemistry. Personal commitment cannot be legislated. Consider arranged marriages. Sometimes they are successful, but without substantial commitment they may be less prone to result in long-term satisfaction. This is not to say that formally assigned mentorships cannot be quite successful. Evidence indicates that they can be. But formal assignment places more burden on the mentor to consistently engage with a mentee even when the "match" appears precarious.

As in other kinds of adult relationships, having the ability to choose a mentoring partner often yields the best outcomes.

Equal access to a mentorship is another important consideration. Gender, race, age, ethnicity, and religion are sometimes important matching concerns (see the next chapter). However, these variables should not be used to limit mentees' opportunities for mentoring. Therefore, mentors should ascertain if they harbor differences or biases that might interfere with their ability to effectively mentor someone who is different. Excellent mentors balance self-awareness and honesty regarding matching preferences with a willingness to ensure fairness and equal access in their selection of mentees. If they do not sense a good match, they may provide assistance to the individual or make suggestions about other potential mentors.

KEY COMPONENTS

- *Choose mentees selectively from among those juniors you come to know informally.*
- *Consider important matching variables when choosing mentees.*
- *Remember that personality, communication style, personal values, and career interests are especially salient matching variables.*
- *Find mentees who share your level of ambition and drive and your interest in balancing career development with friendship and interpersonal sharing.*
- *Balance matching concerns with efforts to ensure that potential mentees from underrepresented groups have a reasonable probability of becoming your mentee.*

38

Clarify Expectations

Alex, a new junior-level manager, immediately impressed David, a senior administrator at a large medical center. Alex was a quick learner, effective manager, and dedicated employee. After several months, David approached Alex about serving as his mentor in the medical center's mentoring program for new hires—hoping to propel Alex expeditiously through the management pipeline. Although he came across as excited about this opportunity, Alex seldom scheduled meetings with David or took the initiative to meet informally. As a result, the two of them had very little interaction at first. David worried about this behavior. He decided to schedule a meeting and inquire about Alex's apparent avoidance. In this meeting, Alex admitted some apprehension about "wasting" David's time. He described a former supervisor who was easily angered by any intrusions. David realized he had neglected to clarify expectations about the mentorship and proceeded to do so. The two agreed to weekly "coffee breaks" and more formal monthly meetings. In addition, David clarified his expectation that Alex would "drop by" anytime he had a need to talk about a question, concern, or idea.

Everyone has expectations—expectations about life, work, and relationships. People have lofty hopes and dreams, anticipate advancements in their careers, and expect to have fulfilling lives. People carry expectations into relationships, and mentorships are no exception. People may be aware of their expectations. But more than we might imagine, they are not consciously aware of what they expect. Yet expectations, whether or not people are aware of them, influence their behavior and interactions with other people.

Some people are astute enough to clarify their expectations and then make them known. On the other hand, many people are not clear about their expectations, let alone clarifying them for relational partners. In mentorships that prematurely terminate, researchers have found that misunderstanding and mismatched assumptions underlie mentorship dysfunction. During the formation stage of a mentorship, outstanding mentors initiate discussions of expectations. They may discuss a range of topics with their mentees. Among the frequent and important topics are the nature of the relationship, roles for each party, responsibilities, frequency of contact, contexts for interaction, and a time frame for ending a formally assigned mentorship or renegotiating the relationship as it evolves and changes. A critical aspect of the discussion is negotiation. Through a process of openness and give-and-take, mentors and their mentees should arrive at clear expectations that are mutually agreed upon.

One item to consider is both parties' previous experiences in mentorships. Previous experiences can exert a powerful influence on a new relationship, but the influence may go unnoticed unless it is openly talked about. Prominent psychologist Robert Sternberg wisely observed that each of us brings to relationships tremendously variable experiences, emotions, motives, and thoughts—our preconceived "story" of what a mentorship should be. This is our *ideal mentor story*, and most of us have one. To establish an effective collaboration, mentors seek to understand the mentee's ideal story. Then they compare that story with their own experiences and their template for what makes a great mentorship work. As conversations unfold, mentors and mentees should begin to appreciate the other's point of view. This is when they negotiate, make concessions, and finally agree on mutually acceptable expectations.

The actual expectations sometimes are less important than the fact that they are discussed openly and made explicit. During the *formation* stage, for instance, frequency of contact is a critical issue. Mentees often want a lot of contact and specific guidance. Perhaps the mentor is often busy or travels frequently; this information must be clarified in advance, along with a clear plan for meeting when time allows. Other expectations to clarify early include credit in shared projects, typical work style, and a mentor's relative strengths and weaknesses (e.g., the mentor is better at giving career advice and less comfortable with offering reassurance and counseling). These steps can prevent misunderstanding and eliminate potential conflict.

The final point to remember is that mentors must take primary responsibility for clarifying expectations. Mentees are understandably novice. They do not have the knowledge and wisdom that mentors have gained through their professional experiences. Mentors initiate the meeting to discuss expectations, and they initiate the actual discussion during the meeting. During the discussion, they communicate with sensitivity. They understand that at this stage in their development, mentees may have significant self-doubts or hesitate to speak up because of the power differential in the relationship. To ensure that no stones are left unturned, mentors should revisit the issue of expectations from time to time.

KEY COMPONENTS

- *Explicitly discuss and clarify your expectations of mentees.*
- *Ask mentees to clarify any expectations for mentoring and for you as a mentor.*
- *Revisit expectations periodically, to both update them and evaluate the extent to which they are being met.*
- *Be particularly careful to clarify expectations about frequency of contact, mentor roles, and mentee performance.*

39
Establish Measurable Goals

If success could be quantified in terms of number of people mentored, then Reggie would be a unanimous all-star selection. A career high school math teacher and engaging mentor, Reggie began each semester asking students to write down their names and what they wanted to be. Over the years, there had been several students who indicated aspirations of becoming astronauts, but something was different about Wendy. Already a solid math student, she sought Reggie out for extra instruction, and as a mentorship developed, she reiterated her intent to become an astronaut. Whereas other students failed to follow through, Wendy never wavered. Her determination was at the forefront of everything she said and everything she did. What she didn't know was how to make it happen. Reggie jumped into action, helping Wendy work backward from her NASA dream to the specific goals and milestones she'd need to achieve en route. Because the Naval Academy placed more students in the space program than any other college, Reggie and Wendy studied the entrance requirements and Wendy then established tangible and measurable goals related to grade point average, SAT scores, leadership positions, varsity athletics, and a congressional nomination. More immediately, she set goals for each year remaining in high school. Whenever possible, specific priority rankings and dates were assigned to each key goal statement. When her letter of appointment to the academy arrived, Wendy was thrilled and immediately began working with Reggie to set goals for her college and early career years.

In the classic movie *What About Bob?* Bill Murray plays a deeply neurotic and chronically anxious man named Bob who can barely manage to leave his apartment without feeling utterly overwhelmed. Bob's psychiatrist, played by Richard Dreyfuss, teaches him to use the "baby steps" technique of setting small and manageable goals. Bob finds significant relief in the strategy of focusing on only one small and attainable objective at a time.

Although most of your mentees will be healthier than Bob, all of them will benefit from the practice of setting and then methodically pursuing goals. Of course, the best goals will be realistic yet ambitious. Effective goals will help both mentor and mentee sharpen a vision for the mentee's development and clarify the purpose of the relationship. Goal-setting should occur early in a mentorship—thus we nest this element in the "Matters of Beginning" section. Nevertheless, goal-setting should occur throughout the relationship as goals set earlier are achieved and the need arises for new goals.

If you are helping someone and yet cannot identify a single goal, either for the relationship itself or for the other person's development, then we challenge you to ask yourself this: *What are you doing?* Mentoring carries an implied commitment to helping the other person grow and develop. This is impossible without some well-defined goals. Similarly, other kinds of meaningful relationships are equally dependent on goals. Although friendships, romances, and parent-child relationships may not meet the technical criteria for mentorships, they often hinge upon a shared vision of the road ahead. By definition, goal-setting is fundamental to healthy relationships.

In element 4, we mentioned the importance of helping mentees to discern, articulate, and ultimately pursue their dreams. Whether the dream involves becoming a neurosurgeon, a first grade teacher, or a mystery writer, the dream probably will not become a reality unless the person methodically achieves a series of smaller objectives. In essence, the dream must be broken into bite-sized pieces. Mentees can easily become disheartened in pursuit of their dreams. The bigger their dreams—and the more obstacles they encounter—the more likely they will hit a period of discouragement. To prevent getting stalled and inoculate against discouragement, they need a plan of action that consists of goals.

Remember this: many mentees have difficulty articulating their precise goals. This is especially true early in the mentoring relationship. Although they may have big dreams and a general sense of what they want personally and professionally, they may lack a specific vision about where they are headed. No wonder that the average college student changes majors several times before finally making a commitment. Here mentors need to be patient. Try using the Socratic questioning technique (see element 24; e.g., "Imagine it is 20 years down the road and you are very happy; what do you envision yourself doing? If you could do anything you wanted with your life, no matter how silly it sounds, what might it be?").

In the early stages of a mentorship, help your mentee craft several crisp goal statements. Some should apply to the next several weeks and months, and some may require a year or more to achieve. Each statement should lead in some way to the dream. Excellent goal statements can create a sense of excitement and purpose. They can cast a clear path and keep the mentee on track. And effective goals bolster a mentee's self-confidence. Keep in mind that excellent goal statements are specific (e.g., publish a short newsletter, score above the eightieth percentile on the Graduate Record Exam (GRE), achieve tenure in the school district, spend 60 minutes every day in aerobic exercise), time determined, and realistic.

Finally, many worthwhile goals are measurable. Because they can be quantified, it's easy to determine when they have been achieved. On the other hand, some worthwhile goals are qualitative and cannot be easily measured (e.g., satisfaction with career, a sense of purpose, work-life balance). Because they are not quantifiable, it's more difficult to determine when they are achieved. Do not jump to the hasty conclusion that quantitative goals are more important than qualitative goals. That is not necessarily true. If a goal is not quantifiable, it may require more specific detail, or subjective ratings may have to suffice. The worst thing you can do is discount the importance of goals that are more difficult to measure.

KEY COMPONENTS

- *Guide your mentees through the process of personal and career goal-setting.*
- *Connect the mentee's dream to specific short- and long-term goals.*
- *Ensure that mentee goals are specific, time determined, realistic, and, as much as possible, measurable.*
- *Be patient and Socratic in helping mentees to articulate career goals.*
- *Collaborate with your mentee on goals for the mentorship itself.*
- *Judge the value of a goal by its importance, not by whether it is easily measurable.*

40

Define Relationship Boundaries

When Greg, a partner at a consulting firm, and Caroline, one of several junior consultants at the firm, began a mentorship, both were concerned about the perceptions others might have of their relationship. They were determined not to let gossip or jealousies keep them from having a productive working relationship. Early in the relationship, they set boundaries. For instance, Greg recommended that they meet only at work and that they hold closed-door meetings only when absolutely necessary. They also agreed not to socialize outside the firm. Fi-

nally, Greg asked Caroline's permission to include a second partner in all decisions regarding her salary and promotion. Greg explained that this safeguard would prevent his strong sense of advocacy for Caroline from unfairly disadvantaging other consultants in the firm.

Healthy mentorships are defined by both what they are and what they are not. The definition of a mentorship may involve the mentor having multiple roles in relation to the mentee. Sometimes the roles overlap, such as work supervisor, performance appraiser, advisor, project collaborator, and friend. Some mentorships may involve interaction in varied settings (office, offsite meetings, travel, and social gatherings). The overlapping roles and varying contexts of mentorship do not need to result in inappropriate behavior or violations of personal boundaries. However, they do call for vigilance on the part of the mentor, as mentorships are not defined as romantic or sexual partnerships. These types of relationships generally compromise the integrity of mentorships.

To avoid overstepping boundaries, mentors must clarify relationship boundaries, and they should do so from the outset of the relationship. Here are important boundary issues to cover:

1. issues of confidentiality;
2. appropriate mediums or contexts for interaction;
3. frequency of contact;
4. acceptability of communication by phone (work and home), email, and social media;
5. rules governing socializing; and
6. a strategy for handling uncomfortable dual roles such as collegial mentor and primary supervisor.

The literature suggests that supervisory mentors, more so than nonsupervisory mentors, must simply remain vigilant against potential harm they may inflict on mentees. The potential for harm is greatest when roles become confused or blurred.

Here is a helpful principle: the more roles added to a mentorship, the greater the risk for crossing boundaries. Here is another principle: the greater the risk for crossing boundaries, the more likely there will be negative outcomes in the mentorship. When mentoring is confined to developing a mentee in a work-related setting, risk of boundary violation is lowest. As the amount of time spent outside the traditional work setting increases and the list of reasons to interact grows, the risk of crossing boundaries also increases. Consider a mentor who becomes a business partner, religious director, psychotherapist, or best friend to a mentee. The potential for confusion and conflict escalates. The "psychotherapist" mentor may discover evidence of emotional disturbance that raises concern about a mentee's suitability for the profession, or the "best friend" mentor may be less able to deliver objective evaluation or needed confrontation. Although some mentors successfully play multiple roles, appreciation for the risks involved should not and cannot be easily dismissed.

No discussion of mentorship boundaries is complete without delving into romantic and sexual intimacies between mentors and mentees. Sexualized mentorships greatly increase the chance of harm while reducing the benefits to the mentee. When a mentorship takes on a sexual dimension, mentors compromise their ability to evaluate the mentee fairly and objectively. Mentees may feel trapped, fearing that their career advancement opportunities rest on yielding to the mentor's romantic or sexual overtures. Also, mentors unwittingly model exploitation and abuse of power. Substantial research shows that mentees who become sexually involved with mentors become angrier and regretful as time goes on. What is initially viewed as "mutual" by the mentee is often seen later as exploitive. We consider sexual relationships with mentees to be *bright-line* boundary violations. They are always exploitive and usually cause harm. A sexualized mentorship should be terminated at once. The mentor should also seek consultation and reevaluate the wisdom of working with mentees until his or her own ethical prudence and respect for professional boundaries are restored.

KEY COMPONENTS
- *Respect relationship boundaries between you and your mentee.*
- *Clarify appropriate contexts for interaction, any limits on confidentiality, and rules regarding socializing outside of the work setting.*
- *Avoid adding new roles (e.g., psychotherapy, business collaboration) to a mentorship.*
- *Refuse to allow a mentorship to become romantic or sexual.*

41

Consider Mentee Relationship Style

When the company human resources director asked Jeffrey to consider serving as a mentor in the new manager mentor program, Jeffrey agreed and looked forward to a new challenge. His first mentee was Jim, a junior scientist from the research and development department. At their first scheduled meeting, Jim was courteous and responsive, yet somewhat uncomfortable as Jeffrey described the typical course of mentorships in the program. During the next year, Jeffrey provided considerable information, teaching, and coaching as Jim began taking on managerial duties. He noticed, however, that Jim became quite uncomfortable when Jeffrey asked him how he was doing personally, tried to engage in small talk, or generally showed an interest in him as a friend. It became obvious Jim preferred only an "exchange of information" when the two met. Although

Jeffrey's mentoring appeared to help Jim understand and navigate company politics and manager requirements, Jeffrey never got the sense that he really "knew" his mentee. He eventually accepted Jim's standoffish style and understood this as Jim's broad approach to relationships. He continued to offer career mentoring without expecting any reciprocal or friendly relationship to develop. When the formal program ended, Jim seldom sought Jeffrey out and the two remained cordial but reserved in their connection.

Your mentorship is not the most important relationship your mentee will ever have. Your mentee's most important relationship began long ago—with parents or guardians. The nature of the relationship undoubtedly has changed over the years, but its effects reach into the mentee's current life. What were the mentee's parents or guardians like? Were they reliable and loving? Did your mentee emerge secure and trusting or disconnected and avoidant? Whatever your mentee's relationship style, remember this: although you had nothing to do with creating it, you had better examine it carefully and tailor your approach to best fit this style.

Famed child development researcher John Bowlby was the first person to demonstrate that children's interactions with their parents, typically during the first year of life, have a profound impact on their interactions with others throughout life. Bowlby's research shows that these early experiences influence the extent to which people seek out relationships, put trust in other people, and develop a defining personality style. Not surprisingly, he found that children who have a secure attachment base develop a sense of trust, and they are not anxious or insecure about undertaking new activities or forming new relationships as adults.

So what does attachment have to do with mentoring? As a mentor, you will likely encounter mentees with one of three attachment or relationship styles. The style will dictate the nature of their receptivity to a mentorship. *Secure* mentees have formed secure and trusting attachments to parents early in life. As mentees, they are likely to be more trusting and comfortable. Secure adults initiate and pursue mentorships more so than people from any other group. They have high self-esteem and are prone to assume that the motivations of others are benevolent. *Avoidant* mentees have not developed secure attachments to primary caregivers in childhood. Consequently, they do not easily trust others and generally spurn close relationships. Although a mentor can help an avoidant individual, it may be difficult to really describe the mentorship as a bonded relationship. *Preoccupied* mentees want closeness and relationships, but they remain unsure about whether they can really rely on others to come through for them. As mentees, they respond with ambivalence to mentoring. On the one hand, they enjoy a mentor's guidance and the care they receive. On the other hand, they fundamentally believe the mentor may prove to be unreliable. These mentees approach mentorship with such caution that they anticipate eventual disappointment with the relationship.

Which of these three relational styles characterizes your mentee? You absolutely need to consider your mentees' relational style as one important facet of their personality. It can dictate the very nature of your relationship. The secure mentee will be engaged and allow the mentorship to unfold in the direction of increasing closeness and collegiality. The preoccupied mentee may initially appear secure but may occasionally withdraw or interpret minor oversights as evidence of mentor unreliability. The avoidant mentee is unlikely to enter into a mentorship in the first place but, in some organizations, may be assigned a formal mentor as part of a larger program.

After considering these relational styles, adjust your expectations and approach mentoring accordingly. Secure mentees can handle the texture and intensity of a healthy relationship. Avoidant mentees can appreciate various career mentoring functions but will be overwhelmed by and actively run away from all things personal or relational. Preoccupied mentees will require the mentor's patience and consistency as they go through periods of ambivalence and retraction from relational connection.

KEY COMPONENTS
- *Remember that mentees bring their own relationship style to the mentorship.*
- *Accept the fact that some mentees will be quite receptive to a relationship while others will be avoidant or ambivalent.*
- *Let the mentee's style guide your approach to mentoring.*
- *Recognize that secure mentees will benefit from career and relational functions while avoidant mentees may only accept career functions.*

42
Describe Potential Benefits and Risks

A famous author and popular professor, Oscar had been nominated for the Pulitzer Prize for his writings on economics. Paradoxically, he also was considered a "thorn" in the university's side. His revolutionary ideas and bombastic style often caused him to be reviled and rejected by colleagues and administrators. Oscar occasionally agreed to mentor a younger "star" in his subspeciality of economics, but whenever he did, he was careful to offer what he called "informed consent." He warned faculty that association with him might "make your career, sink your career, or both!" Oscar elaborated that although he was successful in helping new professors get grants and gain international recognition, association with him also resulted in his mentees' receiving occasional jibes and rejections from colleagues Oscar had alienated. He felt that prospective mentees should understand the assets as well as potential liabilities in committing to a mentorship with him.

Inherent in all mentorships are potential risks and benefits. Some of these consequences are not always apparent. Therefore, as much as possible, mentors should inform mentees about the primary risks and benefits associated with mentoring. In the majority of cases, mentorship outcomes are almost always positive from the mentee's perspective. Salient benefits include more rapid professional development, greater satisfaction with training and one's career, faster promotion rates, larger salaries and total compensation packages, accelerated career mobility, and a stronger sense of competence and confidence in one's job. In short, mentees have more opportunities, are better compensated, and feel more prepared to succeed in their field. Because of these benefits, some professionals believe that identification with a mentor should be considered a major developmental task in one's early career.

Although the benefits usually outweigh the risks in mentor relationships, some risks do exist. Animosity or professional jealousy on the part of peers is a salient risk. The infamous "black halo" effect is another. Here the mentee's career is adversely affected when a mentor falls out of favor in the organization. Then there are the mentorships that turn sour. Here one or both parties feel disenchanted, disappointed, or emotionally wounded, which may occur for a variety of reasons, such as unmet expectations, feelings of abandonment, or jealousy.

Mentors can take a couple of steps to help mentees in this area. First, they can discuss potential risks early in the relationship or even before the mentee commits to the mentorship. This shows respect by giving the mentee an informed choice. An informed mentee may decide that the potential risks are not worth the commitment. On the other hand, an informed mentee is better prepared to help prevent any negative outcomes or handle them if they occur.

Second, mentors can be open and honest about benefits and risks they stand to incur in the relationship. Mentors benefit by increasing their productivity, gaining recognition for their mentoring abilities, and experiencing satisfaction associated with seeing a talented junior professional thrive. Mentoring is often a good way to create a network of good colleagues and friends. Mentors may enjoy years of ongoing collaboration with mentees. Occasionally, successful mentees may even become sources of opportunity and advancement for the mentor.

On the downside, mentors risk guilt by association if the mentee fails or behaves inappropriately. They also risk loss of time and resources if a mentee drops out of a program or organization, does not advance, or fails to live up to expectations. These outcomes would make a mentorship a poor investment. By discussing these issues, mentees can gain a better appreciation for the reciprocal nature of mentorships. They can also gain a better understanding of their responsibility in the relationship. Of course, mentors cannot hold themselves responsible for knowing every possible risk and benefit. Just when you think you have seen it all, an unexpected risk or benefit might surface. The important thing is to be transparent and approach the discussion with an attitude of concern for the mentee.

KEY COMPONENTS

- *Be open and transparent about the benefits and risks of being a mentor.*
- *Discuss the likely benefits of mentoring for the mentee.*
- *Discuss the potential risks of mentoring for the mentee.*

43

Foster Mentoring Constellations

As a senior manager in a midwest company specializing in baking technology, Tom enjoyed many opportunities to mentor junior managers. While he was on the introverted side and very task oriented, Tom was aware of both his mentoring strengths and weaknesses. His assets included teaching, coaching, and challenging his subordinates. His liabilities included his lack of emotional support, unexpressed empathy for his subordinates, as well as the inability to counsel them. Experience, however, had taught Tom an important lesson. His mentees were best served through the mentoring of a collection of senior and experienced professionals—not just one individual. When Tom began mentoring Monique, he clarified at the outset his strong points, the elements of mentoring that he was confident he could deliver. He also indicated his weaknesses and then strongly encouraged Monique—with his assistance—to create a network of career helpers. The network would consist of a cadre of professionals, both internal and external to the company, each of whom could mentor Monique in specific areas for which they had strengths. For instance, when Monique had questions about balancing the competing demands of family and career, Tom—a bachelor—introduced her to a senior female manager who had been successful in this regard. Tom was equally encouraging when Monique established contact with managers in other departments and even other companies. Recognizing the benefit such diverse mentoring contacts could have for Monique, Tom was never jealous of Monique's varied mentor connections.

In common parlance, a *constellation* is a group of stars that are connected in such a way as to form a figure or pattern. A key word in the definition is "connected." Without the participation of the various stars and the way in which they contribute to the constellation, the figure or pattern is incomplete.

Effective mentoring requires the participation of a variety of mentors in the development of mentees. As the saying goes, "You can't do it all." When mentors try to be all things to all mentees—what we refer to as the *guru fantasy*—they are sure to disappoint themselves and those they endeavor to help. Excellent mentors recognize their limitations and the value of a rich network of career helpers.

Research clearly shows that early career professionals with several different developmental relationships (mentorships) enjoy greater career success and satisfaction. Sure, having a primary mentor is critical, but augmenting that relationship with a broader network—a constellation of supportive career helpers, identified in the literature by such names as *developmental networks*, *mentoring constellations*, or *composite mentoring*—creates a distinct advantage. Early in their career, people who have multiple sources of mentoring are more productive, successful, and content with their careers than those who have a single mentor.

The notion of the mentoring constellation is at odds with the common view of a mentor. Underlying the common view is the assumption that a single mentor can and should meet every mentee's developmental needs. But no mentor should fall prey to this guru fantasy. To be competent, a mentor does not have to pretend to be Superman or Superwoman. Instead, a mentor should find it liberating that mentoring constellations can play a vital role in the development of mentees. Although we provide a number of elements of mentoring in this book, we think mentors are most effective when they play to their strengths, seek to develop themselves in their areas of weakness, but never try to be all things to all people.

Here is how you can help your mentees develop their own mentoring constellations. First, introduce them to the concept of a mentoring constellation and explain its benefits. Because the concept will be new to many mentees, they may be surprised at the possibility of having a collection of supportive people who take an interest in their development. Second, encourage your mentees to select these mentors carefully. As the primary mentor, identify your strengths and weaknesses and then assist mentees in searching for individuals who complement you. A diverse network consisting of individuals who have a variety of experiences and strengths is recommended. Third, check your attitude, and never undermine mentees' efforts at constructing career-helping networks. There is no room for petty jealousy or territoriality when it comes to your mentees. Mentoring always is about maximizing mentee success, not gratifying your ego by causing mentees to focus their attention exclusively on you.

Finally, there are other types of relationships you could encourage that aid in the development of mentees. For instance, peer mentoring (supportive relationships between persons at the same career stage), group mentoring (formally or informally arranged meetings with several persons interested in career and personal support), and e-mentoring/virtual mentoring (mentoring assistance established in online networks designed for early career professionals). The keys to establishing these relationships include ensuring that they augment the existing mentoring and that they are undertaken with an intentional commitment to the mentee's development.

KEY COMPONENTS

- *Encourage your mentees to develop networks of career helpers.*
- *Refuse to become jealous or territorial of mentees' other mentoring connections.*

- *Appreciate the added value that composite mentoring brings to mentees.*
- *Encourage mentees to seek mentors with diverse backgrounds and experience.*

44

Plan for Change at the Outset

During the first few months of their developing mentorship, Gail and Shannon had frequent interaction, a strong sense of "synergy" or creative excitement about various investigative writing projects, and a mutual sense that the relationship would be both productive and enjoyable. As a senior overseas correspondent for a major newspaper, Gail occasionally mentored well-matched junior journalists assigned to her foreign office headquarters. These mentorships were meaningful and career enhancing. But Gail had learned that the company generally rotated new journalists back to New York after three years. For this reason, Gail was careful to discuss this eventuality with Shannon and to predict at the outset of the relationship that the two of them might only be able to work actively together for about three years. The two discussed in advance how they would honor and celebrate Shannon's transition to new responsibilities and, if both agreed, how they would redefine their relationship and perhaps continue collaborating in some form.

From the beginning of the relationship, mentors should plan for the development, change, and eventual ending of the formal aspect of the mentorship. Early in the formation of a mentorship, both the mentor and mentee experience excitement, synergy, and some degree of mutual need fulfillment; both anticipate the benefits to come from the relationship. From this early vantage point, however, it may be difficult to soberly anticipate the changes necessary for maximal health and usefulness. By definition, mentorships are developmental relationships. If the mentee does not change, mature, and ultimately require less formal mentoring, something is drastically wrong. As in healthy parent-child relationships or marriages, good mentorships adapt to the changing circumstances and needs of the partners. Otherwise, they risk stagnation and disintegration.

As a benchmark, traditional mentorships in business and management settings endure for an average of five years. In actuality, there is wide variation in the actual length of specific mentorships. Some terminate after several months of intense collaboration, while others last for decades after the most active phase of the mentorship has ended. Sometimes, only the mentor's death brings an end to a mentorship (and research demonstrates that the example, wisdom, and encouragement of excellent mentors continue to positively influence mentees long after the mentor's death).

Regardless of their duration, many mentorships proceed through four predictable yet somewhat overlapping phases. During the *initiation* phase, the mentor and mentee get to know each other, begin working together, and commence a mentoring relationship. The *cultivation* (active) phase is characterized by much of the active and intensive mentoring that will occur in the relationship. During this stage the mentor typically provides the widest range of mentor functions beginning with career functions (coaching, teaching, sponsoring) and also including psychosocial functions (support, encouragement, and friendship). During the cultivation period, mentors and mentees must give up their idealizations—both of each other and of the mentorship. They have to accept the realistic limitations of mentorship, perhaps allowing their ideal views to give way to a good or adequate view of the relationship. The point is that they must let reality set in.

In the *separation* phase, the nature of the mentorship is substantially altered by structural changes in the organization (typically, one or both parties move on) or by psychological and developmental changes within one or both individuals. At times, these changes are anticipated. At other times, these changes come about suddenly, catching either party or both parties off guard. Finally, if the mentorship does not end entirely during the separation phase, it will enter the final phase, known as *redefinition*. Here the mentorship evolves into an entirely new shape and form. The interaction is less intense, and the parties experience more collegiality. We should note that, while these phases are useful guides, they are approximations and do not apply equally across mentorships.

Mentors should anticipate change at the outset and work with mentees to plan flexible time frames for the transitions and even termination of the mentorship. They should discuss the desirable milestones (e.g., graduation, promotion, assignment to a different division, or the mentee's sense of increased confidence and preference for increasing independence) that might signal to both the mentor and mentee that the relationship requires redefinition. They also should take the lead in narrating these changes as they occur (e.g., "You know, you're really becoming more independent. I'm impressed with your confidence. I notice that you don't need my advice so much these days—a sign you are mastering your work! Although I'll miss our close work together, I'm delighted to see you succeed and move ahead").

An inevitable consequence of redefinition and separation are some feelings of loss. And separation can be difficult for both the mentee and mentor, depending on the intensity of the relationship, their bonding, and their sense of fulfillment and achievement. The actual experience of loss, therefore, varies from mentorship to mentorship. The helpful and healthy action to take is to acknowledge up front the inevitability of separation, accepting that life is unpredictable, that the mentorship may endure in some form for a time, that it may end prematurely due to circumstances beyond either party's control, or that the mentorship has become unproductive or harmful.

Concerned mentors help mentees work through their feelings of loss. It might be helpful for them to assist their mentees in moving through the stages of grief associated with relationship endings. A number of self-help resources are useful to this end. In addition, mentors may need to work through their own feelings of loss. One of the most trying experiences of parenthood is separation from children and the subsequent empty-nest syndrome. The child does not cease to exist but may be moving on to a life of personal fulfillment. Still, there is loss, melancholy, and a sense of something missing. In a similar vein, a mentee's development and separation can have a strong emotional impact on the mentor. The separation from a mentee may surface a full spectrum of emotions, including relief, joy, gratitude, and sadness. It is in the mentor's best interest to acknowledge these emotions and find ways to manage them constructively. Otherwise, the mentor may become overwhelmed and mishandle the separation.

KEY COMPONENTS

- *Understand that mentorships travel through predictable phases, including initiation, cultivation, separation, and redefinition.*
- *Plan for and welcome growth in your mentee as well as transitions in the relationship.*
- *Discuss relationship changes as they occur and find ways to recognize and honor them.*
- *Accept the emotional side of mentorship separation and ending.*

45

Schedule Periodic Reviews or Evaluations

A high school principal and prolific mentor, James typically had two or three "rising star" teachers whom he mentored. His mentees moved to leadership positions in the school and, ultimately, in the larger school district. Known for his personal organization and attention to detail, James kept files on his mentees for the purpose of documenting their career goals and tracking their progress. As soon as James determined that a mentorship was forming, he scheduled a formal meeting with the teacher, explained that he was willing to serve as a guide and sponsor to promote and support the person's career development, and inquired about their aspirations and ideal career trajectory. He then used this information to guide them toward relevant teaching experiences, appropriate graduate courses, and key committee assignments. Twice annually, he would meet with each of his mentees to monitor their career progress and evaluate the quality and value of the mentorship.

As the mentorship begins, it is often helpful to develop an intentional plan for review and evaluation. When both parties actively participate in a systematic process of evaluation, tangible progress toward the mentee's professional development can be assessed and then celebrated. This formative process of evaluation typically does not need to be overly technical, laborious, or formal, although greater structure and formality are necessary in some contexts. Mentors should take the lead in discussing the significance of periodic evaluations and then tentatively schedule appointments for the purpose of mutual review and evaluation of the mentorship. More frequent evaluation often is helpful early in the relationship (e.g., every three to six months), while more mature mentorships may require less frequent evaluation (e.g., annually or less often if the separation phase has already occurred). When the mentor emphasizes goal-setting and subsequent assessment, the mentee becomes more attuned to outcomes and more prone to intentionally consider ideal mentorship outcomes.

What should be reviewed or evaluated by mentor and mentee? Some salient questions to ask: Is the mentorship meeting both participants' primary needs (e.g., encouragement, support, coaching, assistance with research, collegiality)? Is the mentee making progress toward both short- and long-term career goals? Are there sources of conflict, frustration, or stress in the mentorship, and how can these be addressed? Does either party feel that his or her main expectations or hopes for the mentorship are not materializing? Why or why not? What can be done to address this situation? Have circumstances, interests, or needs changed such that the mentorship must transition to a different form or begin the process of ending?

Periodic and planned discussions of a mentorship help to ensure that the relationship is maintained, transformed, or dissolved if this is necessary. Planned reviews and evaluations, when initiated by the mentor, also serve as powerful models for the mentee. It shows responsible and committed professionalism as well as a personal commitment to serve the best interests of the mentee. It cannot be overemphasized that evaluations will only occur if the mentor makes them a priority. Discussing this at the outset, scheduling and following through with reflective conversations, and making subsequent adjustments demonstrate ethical and responsible mentoring practice.

If you plan to mentor a number of mentees over a period of years, perhaps even over the course of a long career, we recommend broader evaluation of your mentoring efficacy. First, consider collecting some standard data from mentees at distinct junctures in their careers. For example, you might keep track of your mentees' jobs, their records of achievement in the field, their level of compensation, and their level of satisfaction with their career and with their mentorship experience. When aggregated across a number of mentees, such data will be useful to you and perhaps to the organization that employs you. For instance, some universities have commenced discussion about how to routinely evaluate faculty efficacy in the domain of student mentorship. Consider how you might systematically assess your mentoring endeavors without making the process onerous or losing your focus on mentee development. Depending on the nature of the data you collect, it additionally may shed light on your particular strengths and weaknesses as a mentor—offering grist for the self-improvement mill.

Second, periodically ask mentees for their feedback during the active phase of your mentorship. Mentors should solicit mentees' ideas on what is helpful and what is not. The important point is that the mentor takes the mentee seriously and remains open to the feedback. In general, mentees will not be put off by requests for feedback and assessment. To the contrary, they are likely to appreciate the mentor's interest in improving the mentorship.

KEY COMPONENTS
- *Develop a plan for periodic review and evaluation of your mentorship.*
- *Work with your mentee to determine career goals and mentorship expectations and ways to evaluate progress toward meeting each.*
- *Review the mentorship more frequently at the outset and less frequently as the mentorship matures.*
- *Use periodic evaluation to determine the direction mentoring should take.*
- *Consider a strategy for evaluating your mentoring outcomes across mentees and over time.*

Celebrating Diversity

MATTERS OF HUMAN DIFFERENCES

Master mentors appreciate and honor cultural differences. Simply observe how they initiate and manage mentorships with mentees from diverse racial, ethnic, religious, gender, sexual orientation, age, and other groups. These mentors understand that culturally diverse organizations that also effectively develop the talent among their ranks become strong, vibrant, and competitive. They come to understand that mentoring along the lines of diversity builds their competence as a mentor. At the same time, they come to a sobering realization that people often prefer to engage with certain types of people, especially those who look just like them or share similar backgrounds and value orientations. For this reason, they are judicious and deliberate about mentoring diverse mentees. Each of the seven elements in this section hones in on the salient components of celebrating human differences.

As we shall see, outstanding mentors get to know their mentees as whole people, not as individuals who fit into a predetermined cultural, gender, or racial box. With skill and sensitivity, they celebrate each mentee's unique heritage and group identification. This ties in with their cultural humility. They avoid making assumptions about mentees, maintain an interpersonal stance that is genuinely other-oriented, and refrain from labeling themselves "mentor" before a mentee chooses to define their relationship as a mentorship. To ensure equal access and opportunity, they make themselves approachable and available to prospective mentees from various cultural groups. Because of their attunement to the unique needs of underrepresented groups, they channel their energies into being an ally. As allies, they monitor their own biases and prejudices so as not to treat their mentees unfairly. But they go a step further by confronting systemic inequities that interfere with their mentees' success. They are just as thoughtful in applying the above principles to their cross-gender mentorships. In essence, they operate by this mantra: "All mentees are created equal and deserve equal opportunity for professional growth and development." With that thought in mind, as an ongoing practice, they check and double-check themselves to see that all mentees receive the fair and equitable treatment they justly deserve.

46

Honor and Celebrate Differences

Michelle sometimes shook her head and wondered how she and her mentee Michael had managed to forge such a close mentoring bond. As an African American, a lesbian, a secularist, and a woman from an impoverished inner-city background, Michelle had initially struggled to avoid making assumptions about Michael, a white, heterosexual, devoutly Catholic male from an economically privileged part of the city. As principal in the high school where Michael was a new teacher, Michelle had early recognized Michael's passion for teaching science, and a mentorship slowly evolved. At first, Michelle struggled to see Michael as more than a privileged white male. But owing to her expressions of positive regard and encouragement, Michael began dropping by her office with questions about how best to understand and effectively reach his inner-city students. As the pair became more comfortable with each other, they shared more about their backgrounds and cultural identifications. At times, they enjoyed good humor about their differences while recognizing their shared commitment to students. At all times, they showed respect for one another. As the relationship flourished, Michelle attended the christening for Michael's first child, while Michael and his wife invited Michelle and her partner to dinner on occasion. Both would proudly exclaim that their mentorship served to create genuine appreciation for their cultural differences.

In our increasingly global community, cultural differences between mentors and mentees have become more commonplace. Many mentors inevitably enter into mentorships with mentees of different racial, ethnic, cultural, religious, gender, sexual orientation, age, or other lifestyle groups. In the midst of this diversity, mentors should honor and celebrate their mentees' differences. For some mentors, this element is novel because they have never considered this type of celebration. For other mentors, they simply find it easier to avoid broaching any reference to differences. Broaching the topic evokes anxiety. They would rather say nothing and do nothing, knowing that the path of least resistance keeps them safely in their comfort zone.

What does it mean to honor and celebrate differences? These acts are more than the display of fair treatment, although fairness is involved, and they are more than the acknowledgment of differences, although this helps to build the relationship. Honoring and celebrating differences are overt expressions of appreciation for the mentee's one-of-a-kind personhood and the benefits this brings to the mentorship. These expressions are markers of sincerity, affirmation, and joyfulness. They may appear, for instance, as giving kudos in appreciation of mentees' uniqueness in private and in public, encouraging others to value mentees' uniqueness, or joining mentees in their cultural activities. Excellent mentors deliberately add to their growing fund of knowledge about the historical experiences and values of different minority groups while they attempt to discover the unique concerns and developmental needs of each of their culturally different mentees.

Why do mentors honor and celebrate differences? We turn to anthropologists Clyde Kluckhohn and Henry Murray for an answer. In a paraphrase of their famous quote, these authors said, "All people are like all other people, like some other people, and like no other people." This statement succinctly pinpoints the *tripartite* nature of the human experience: *universal*, *group*, and *individual*. First, everyone is a member of the human race, which means that each person has in common with others some physical and psychological endowments. On this basis, the person is like everyone else. Second, everyone holds membership in social groups, such as family, race, faith community, gender, or culture. On this basis, the person is like some other people, but not all. Third, everyone has a unique set of personality traits and interests that separate the person from all other people, even the people with whom they share group membership. On this basis, the person has an individual identity. A hallmark of effective mentorship is the capacity and the willingness to see and appreciate mentees individually rather than merely as representative of their gender, sexual orientation, or racial group. In essence, honoring and celebrating differences validates the total experience of what it means to be human.

Culturally attuned mentors begin by examining their own tripartite identities. The self-examination frees them to celebrate their mentees' tripartite identities without prejudice or bias. Unaware mentors, on the other hand, are more likely to become defensive if mentees indicate concern about their differences. To continue, mentors intentionally create a safe space for appreciating differences. In this context, mentees do not have to defend their identities or worry that some aspects of their identity are acceptable, and other aspects are not. Mentors then can inquire directly to see if mentees have concerns about their differences and whether these might impact the mentorship. Their inquiries must be genuine, and responses to mentees must be nonjudgmental. Finally, mentors point out how the differences enhance the relationship and are vital to their mentees' development. These steps constitute the honor and celebration of differences.

KEY COMPONENTS

- *Look at yourself as a whole person.*
- *Look at each mentee as a whole person.*
- *Think of memorable ways to honor and celebrate differences.*
- *Find out from mentees their perceptions of how the differences affect the mentorship.*

47

Practice Cultural Humility

A white engineer and manager for a research and development lab in a small northwest tech company, Craig began to supervise Derek, one of the firm's newest engineers. To his knowledge, Derek was the only African American engineer in the lab and one of the few in the entire company. Although he often wondered about Derek's experience as an African American man in a predominantly white company and in a part of the state with relatively little racial diversity, Craig was initially reluctant to broach the topic of culture with Derek. As their relationship evolved and Craig began to become a strong advocate and encourager for Derek, he began to ask questions signaling genuine interest in Derek's experience and openness to discussing the topics of race and cultural experience generally (e.g., "I'm curious about how it's going for you as the only African American guy in the lab and one of the few in town. Is there anything we can do better when it comes to being inclusive here?"). Picking up on Craig's genuine interest in understanding his perspective, Derek gradually began to self-disclose about his cultural experiences.

Sometimes mentors hesitate or even avoid entering into mentorships with mentees from other cultures. They may fear they lack the competence to mentor across cultures, or, worse, they fear appearing to be culturally incompetent. Perhaps they previously stumbled in a cross-cultural relationship by saying or doing something that was insensitive and offensive. Perhaps they heard that same-race or same-gender mentorships are preferable, which causes them to question whether they could ever measure up. Whatever the sources of hesitation or avoidance, the real obstacle in cross-cultural mentorships often lies in mentors. They are the ones who must come to terms with their apprehensions in order to meet the needs of mentees from other groups.

A growing body of research suggests that *cultural humility* is an antidote to professionals who fear they lack or appear to lack cultural competence. Cultural humility is the ability of mentors to maintain a stance in relationships that is other-oriented. As in any professional relationship in which there is a power differential, the mentor's stance demonstrates openness to aspects of their mentees' culture that are important to them. The openness of the mentor obviously should benefit the mentee. Incidentally, humility and openness may enrich the experience of the mentor as well.

In the previous element—"Honor and Celebrate Differences"—we discussed the importance of mentors' inquiring about mentees' tripartite identities. In this element, we explain how the openness associated with cultural humility allows for productive inquiry. Mentors do not have all the knowledge and understanding that is vital to mentoring. Despite being in the one-up position—when it comes to technical and professional skills—mentors in cross-cultural mentorships have a need that only their mentees can fulfill. They need to gain a more in-depth understanding of their mentees, especially in that they are products of their cultures. In an interesting reversal of roles, mentees are cast into a position of teaching their mentors. Mentees alone are the experts of their cultural experiences. It is this expertise on culture that mentees need to teach their mentors.

This situation raises the all-important questions: Who is the mentor? And who is the mentee? Unless mentees benefit from the technical and professional expertise of their mentors, they are less likely to reach their maximal potential. Unless mentors benefit from the cultural expertise of their mentees, they are less likely to help their mentees reach their maximal potential. Ultimately, mentors are tasked with the responsibility of making the mentorship a productive experience. They have to gain insights into the cultural experience of their mentees and then utilize what they learn to facilitate the mentees' development. In essence, cultural humility is the willingness of mentors to acknowledge their limitations and become students of their mentees.

Cultural humility has a threefold requirement. First, it requires mentors to have a teachable spirit. This spirit embodies their attitudes, dispositions, and entire orientation to mentoring. Second, it requires mentors to be proactive in the pursuit of opportunities for cross-cultural mentoring. They should set this as a priority rather than passively wait until an opportunity presents itself. Third, cultural humility requires mentors to modify their mentoring practices to accommodate the cultural needs of their mentees. Along the similar lines of honoring and celebrating differences, they must deliberately incorporate cultural considerations into their mentoring.

Here is a final word of wisdom bearing on humility: Unless

your organization has a formal mentoring system or protocol, do not identify yourself as a mentor or label a helping relationship with a junior person as a "mentorship." Instead, allow mentees to assign this or other labels identifying you as a key source of help and inspiration. The need for this wisdom is especially poignant for mentees of color who may be acutely conscious of legacies of oppression. When a senior privileged person (e.g., a white male) claims mentor status with a minority person, the assertion may unintentionally signal ownership and imply an obligation for loyalty. It is also, quite simply, presumptuous. Do the work of mentoring, but remain humble about how your mentees frame your contribution to their development. To coin a phrase: *You are a mentor when your mentee calls you a mentor.*

KEY COMPONENTS
- *Ask yourself if you are other-oriented.*
- *Make yourself a learner.*
- *Incorporate cultural considerations into mentoring.*
- *Unless defined as such in a formal mentoring program, avoid self-identifying as a mentor; let your mentee determine when or if to call you a mentor.*

48

Ensure Equal Access and Opportunity

Fresh from a master's degree program in management, Candice accepted a full-time position in the business department of a local community college. Although the college was located in a reasonably diverse community, Candice was troubled one day when it occurred to her that nearly all of the business students she mentored and pushed forward for admission to the state university's business program were—like her—white. Upon reflection, she realized that students of color were less likely to pursue her for advice and conversation. But if she was honest, she suspected she took less initiative to engage with racially different students and invite out-of-class interaction. She resolved to become more mindful about the demographic makeup of her mentee cohort and deliberate in striking up relationships with and sponsoring racially diverse students.

Dr. Martin Luther King Jr. once said, "Injustice anywhere is a threat to justice everywhere. We are caught in an inescapable network of mutuality tied in a single garment of destiny. Whatever affects one directly affects all indirectly." Although we have made progress since he uttered those profound words during the civil rights movement, the job of ensuring equal access and opportunity is far from completed.

Injustice, inequity, and discrimination—the pentacles of unfairness—come in many forms. Prominent among them are racism, sexism, homophobia, and ageism. While each one of these forms of mistreatment targets a specific group in the population, they share in common one notable feature: the systematic perpetuation of access and opportunity to members of one group and simultaneous denial of access and opportunity to members of the mistreated group. Although we now have civil rights laws that stop many injustices, some covert injustices still fly under our radar screens.

The glass ceiling is a case in point of covert injustice. Marilyn Loden introduced the glass ceiling metaphor to describe a particular type of sexism that prevents women from advancing beyond a certain level on the organizational ladder. Breaking the glass ceiling has been especially difficult for minority women, who have a double minority status. Research evidence suggests that even when women do secure a mentorship, they often reap fewer benefits from the relationship.

How can you help to ensure equal access to mentorship in your setting? Begin with some honest self-reflection. Make a list of everyone you are currently mentoring. Once completed, review the list and ask yourself this question: Do all or most of your mentees look the same? Do they tend to reflect your own demographic profile? If your current cadre of mentees is not varied and inclusive when it comes to race, gender, sexual orientation, and other key cultural variables, perhaps you have some work to do when it comes to deliberately initiating relationships with culturally different mentees. And remember this: access alone does not equate to *opportunity*. If your minority status mentees are less likely to be tabbed for key collaborations, networking events, and promotion opportunities, ask yourself whether the quality and intensity of mentorship is fair across cultural groups.

KEY COMPONENTS
- *Fixate the definition of injustice in your mind.*
- *Determine what other injustices exist in your organization besides the glass ceiling.*
- *Frequently reflect on the cultural diversity among those you mentor.*
- *Consider whether or not culturally different persons have equivalent access to you as a potential mentor.*

49

Be an Ally and an Advocate

When Tony became the newest senior manager for a Silicon Valley software company, he made it a priority to increase the company's retention of talented female and racial minority programmers. Not only did he go out of his way to strike up mentoring relationships with women and people of color when they joined his department, he took a personal interest in them. Specifically, he asked them about their experiences and listened intently to better understand their perspectives on obstacles to promotion and career success. When several of these mentees raised concerns about pay inequity, Tony lobbied for a thorough and public review of salaries in the company. This process led to the revelation of some dramatic pay disparities primarily associated with gender and race. Tony then worked with the executive leadership to immediately close the salary gaps. Furthermore, he collaborated with the leadership to implement transparent review policies. These steps were taken to ensure that similar disparities would not occur in the future.

Are you an ally for mentees from historically nonprivileged groups (race, gender, sexual orientation, religion, etc.)? Recent research reveals that becoming an ally in the eyes of minority groups is harder than it sounds. In their research on the subject, social psychologist Kendrick Brown and his colleagues conclude that an *ally* is an individual not only committed to *expressing* as little prejudice as possible but also invested in *addressing* social inequality. This means that there are two distinct and equally important aspects to becoming a strong ally for cultural minority group mentees.

The first aspect of ally-ship involves working to end prejudice in your personal and professional life. This involves each of the elements covered thus far in this section. Strong allies honor and celebrate their mentees' unique cultural experience and differences. They approach their mentees with a learning orientation and a palpable sense of humility regarding all that they do not know about their mentees' experiences. They are deliberate in initiating mentoring relationships with diverse mentees and then ensuring that those mentees derive the same opportunities from the relationship as do their majority group peers. Finally, they persistently work at understanding their lingering cultural biases and ensuring that these do not lead to prejudicial and discriminatory outcomes in their own relationships.

The second aspect of being an ally to minority group mentees requires a mentor to become a courageous advocate in publically addressing inequity and injustice in the organization or profession. Effective dominant-group mentors consciously use the social privilege conferred by their group status to create opportunity for nondominant group mentees. They do this primarily by actively and publically supporting mentees. A genuine ally is also willing to take *action*, either interpersonally or in the broader setting. Sure, mentors should make certain that they treat their mentees justly. Sure, they should teach mentees to be assertive in the face of injustice and stand up for their rights. But their most important responsibility is to be a systems interventionist. Mentors need to get out of their offices, confront the systemic dynamics within their organizations, and stand as vocal advocates for change. Understandably, confronting practices that challenge the status quo can be costly. Yet the extent to which they do nothing makes them complicit with the problem.

To show that you are a serious ally and advocate, make yourself the local watchdog for disparities. In your workplace and profession, set yourself apart from those who do not have the backbone to take a stand. Take your stand in an assertive but not abrasive manner. Ask yourself questions along these lines. Are female mentees consistently underpaid? Are the contributions and accomplishments of African American mentees typically overlooked, minimized, or discounted? Does homophobic banter in the breakroom leave LGBT mentees feeling marginalized and unwelcomed? If the answers require action, inaction is not a viable option.

KEY COMPONENTS

- *Recognize that effective allies work at eliminating prejudice in their own mentoring relationships while simultaneously advocating for systemic equity and justice.*
- *Take action to ensure equal access and opportunity outside your mentoring relationships.*
- *Get out of your office and publically address disparities for cultural minorities.*
- *If your background is one of privilege, use it advantageously as an ally and advocate.*

50

Appreciate and Honor Gender Differences

Although Andrew frequently mentored junior managers, he was stumped and—to be honest—more than a little anxious when Amy was assigned to him through the manufacturing company's formal mentoring program. Not only was Andrew inexperienced at working with women, he worried that he might say or do something offensive. Andrew was confident enough to share these worries with Amy. To his delight, this bold step increased the trust between them and strengthened their alliance. Andrew soon noticed that Amy encountered a number of slights, more than was typical in their facility. She was dismissed, talked over, or given assignments below her qualifications. He was correct in attributing the mistreatment to gender bias in their male-dominated environment. To show appreciation and honor her, Andrew did several things of significance. He directly intervened when she was mistreated. He affirmed her collegial, democratic style of leadership. And he shared with Amy that he learned as much from her as he believed she ever learned from him.

Is it possible to effectively mentor someone of a different gender? Here is what the research tells us. Cross-gender mentorships tend to form slower than same-gender mentorships. But once they lift off, these mentorships are as effective or even *more so* in producing career-altering outcomes—especially for female mentees. Cross-gender mentorships can produce a powerful synergy as mentor and mentee bring different but complementary strengths and perspectives to the relationship and the tasks at hand. Yet cross-gender mentorships present a number of unique relational complexities and risks. Therefore, mature and thoughtful mentors ensure equal access to mentees of any gender. In the balance of this element, we focus our attention on why and how men should deliberately mentor women. In doing so, we borrow liberally from Brad Johnson and David Smith's book *Athena Rising*.

Mentoring research leaves little doubt. Both men and women can benefit substantially from effective mentoring. But here is the problem: women face far more hurdles to securing mentorship, and even when they do, they typically reap fewer tangible rewards. Part of the problem in many professions is a lack of senior women available to serve as mentors. A bigger slice of the problem is the reluctance on the part of some men to mentor women. So the important question is this: Why do men hang around on the sidelines leaving junior women unsponsored? The answer is complex and multidimensional. Some men don't have much professional experience working with women, nor do they feel comfortable in nonsexual intimate relationships with women. Some worry they'll say or do something that gets them into hot water, while still others feel anxious about misperceptions and gossip that might circulate around the office. And thanks to how men are socialized, many of them harbor implicit biases about women (e.g., "She's a bad investment, she'll leave to have a family; I can't give her honest feedback or she'll become emotional; she seems nice, but I don't see much leadership potential").

What's the solution? Exposure! Rather than quarantine women from male mentorship for fear of rumors, attraction, or making a misstep, men need to initiate *more* interaction and mentorship with women. Mere exposure, sincere gender humility, and a learning orientation will work wonders in lowering anxiety. It's classic psychology 101. Expose people to the objects they fear or bring them anxiety, prevent them from avoiding the objects, and extinction (of the anxiety) occurs: those nagging feelings go away because we are not wired to maintain them in the face of prolonged and intense exposure. And here's an insider note to men: if you mentor women often and deliberately, you benefit as well. Evidence suggests that not only can the mentorship make a huge difference in your career, it can improve your own emotional intelligence, communication skill set, and professional network. To tell the truth, you'll probably also become a better partner, husband, and friend—in a word, an all-around better *man*.

What about the other side of the coin? Can women mentor men? *Undoubtedly and resoundingly: yes.* Interestingly, the original story of mentorship from Greek mythology reveals that Mentor, an older man, was a rather ineffective guide and champion. In truth, it was the goddess Athena, appearing in Mentor's form, who provided most of the powerful guidance, encouragement, and support for Telemachus. According to the research, female mentors tend to do a better job mentoring holistically in that they consider both a mentee's professional *and* personal aspirations. Traditionally, men have been more competitive than women, task-focused, and likely to define their identity in terms of work success. But increasingly, men struggle to balance devotion to work and family, while their career success is measured in part by their mastery of soft skills (e.g., listening, empathy), qualities women are more likely to contribute to a mentoring relationship.

In summary, here are a few things men and women should keep in mind when it comes to mentoring across gender. First, be deliberate and intentional in forming mentorships with the opposite sex and with talented junior colleagues whose gender identity is different from yours. Remember: frequent and sustained exposure is the only solution to overcoming anxiety about the unknown. Second, be humble about what you don't understand about your mentee's gendered experiences. Maintain a transparent, curious, and open learning orientation. Third, watch your own *gender scripts*. If you are a male who ordinarily seeks the role of rescuer for women, be careful about overprotecting female mentees, thereby undermining their autonomy. If you are a female who often assumes a maternal role with young men, be careful about failing to challenge and confront them when needed. Fourth, anticipate attraction, which is quite natural and even inevitable at times in cross-gender mentorships. But allow good judgment, not the attraction, to dictate your behavior. Set strong boundaries and consult with colleagues as deterrents to sexual or romantic involvement with mentees; crossing boundaries is never in your mentee's best interest. Finally, savor the reciprocity, mutuality, and synergy that often accompany learning from a different gender.

KEY COMPONENTS

- *Be attuned to the effects of gender in mentoring relationships.*
- *Deliberately seek out gender-different mentees.*
- *Approach your mentee's gender experience with humility and openness.*
- *Be a watchdog for gender disparities in the workplace and publically address them.*
- *Accept that attraction is common, but do not sexualize or romanticize a mentorship.*

51

Do Not Overburden
Minority Mentees

When the humanities department at a small northeastern private college succeeded in hiring Loretta, an African American, as a new assistant professor of history, both the college and the department celebrated the hire as evidence of progress. At long last, the predominantly white institution evidenced movement toward reaching its diversity goals. But during her first semester on campus, Loretta quickly was overwhelmed by the expectation that she serve on a wide range of diversity and inclusion committees and by the implicit expectation within her department that she would mentor most of the students of color who were humanities majors. She was even called upon to take a significant role when the regional accreditation body visited the college; the college president was eager to showcase the school's newest minority hire. Fortunately for Loretta, her faculty mentor, a senior professor of English, quickly recognized how Loretta was becoming overburdened and spoke with the dean about how exploiting Loretta in this way could ultimately sabotage Loretta's scholarship and her academic promotion. Her mentor also helped her to formulate a strategy for setting limits on future requests for institutional service.

In real life, burden-bearing is natural and normal. We are designed to carry physical loads, mental loads, and relational loads. Carrying loads for various purposes enables us to meet the challenges of everyday living. Burden-bearing also creates stamina and strength, although it has some limits. Carrying too heavy of a load or too often carrying loads is *overburden*. These experiences are neither natural nor normal. Over time, overburden causes a breakdown. The breakdown can be in the physical realm, mental realm, relational realm, or a combination of these. This is the inevitable consequence of going against the natural and normal. And no one is exempt.

Overburden can manifest itself in the extreme expectations that organizations sometimes place on minorities in order to fulfill their mission of equity in the workplace and promote their diversity agenda. To be sure, these are worthy aspirations. Whenever a minority group is underrepresented in an organization or members of the group are found primarily in lower-level positions, we are apt to encounter the politics of equitable treatment and diverse representation. The organization seeks to present the appearance of equity and diversity in its affairs and operations, but the presentation is merely an illusion. True equity and diversity does not actually exist.

The politics of equity and diversity is a setup for overburdening minority mentees—the default option for an organization falling short on its proclamations. One manifestation is the expectation of the *minority model*. This person is exalted as an exemplar of what it means to be a "good" minority—someone for other minorities to emulate. Ironically, this individual may have to outperform majority counterparts to earn equal status while breeding contempt among "lesser good" minorities. Ibram Kendi coined the idea *uplift suasion* as reference to blacks who attempt to outdo racism due their education and moral uprightness. The expectation comes from blacks and whites. Another manifestation is the expectation of the *spokesperson minority*. The spokesperson is the exalted expert on minority affairs and the one who is summoned as the mouthpiece for the entire group. The expectation is especially apparent during periods of strained intergroup relationships. Ironically, the spokesperson minority typically is chosen by the majority group, not the minority group for whom the person supposedly is the mouthpiece. A third manifestation is the expectation of the *minority representative*. This person is expected to participate broadly in organizational affairs and activities. Taking excessive assignments on committees or projects is commonplace. After all, every committee needs representation. Ironically, the minority representative cannot legitimately meet the broad range of expertise required to fulfill the role.

Mentors must protect their minority mentees from these unfair incursions. They are the ones who must discern the politics, call them to the attention of their minority mentees, and fend them off. Mentors must also educate their mentees about the harmful consequences of yielding to these expectations, for these entrapments create an illusion of representativeness that does not exist in reality. The entrapments send a message to minorities that it is their responsibility to be overburdened, and they instill in them a false sense of importance. Additionally, they compromise mentees' careers by interfering with their professional development, hindering their potential for advancement, or circumscribing them in minority-only functions. Finally, they teach stakeholders from majority groups to be insensitive to the realities of the minority experience. Collectively, the consequences of overburdening minority mentees serve as a recipe for burnout.

In addition to the direct protection they provide from overburdening minority mentees, mentors should address the bigger problem. There simply aren't enough minorities in the organization. By advocating for the hiring, retention, and promotion of more minority group members, mentors are indirectly protecting their mentees from overburden.

KEY COMPONENTS
- *Understand the hidden politics of equity and diversity.*
- *Be vigilant for three manifestations of burdening minority mentees.*

- *Remember the costs involved in overburdening minority mentees.*
- *Whenever possible, help minority mentees sidestep minority model, spokesperson, or representative roles.*

52
Check Yourself for Unintentional Bias

An experienced creative director at a New York advertising agency, Adrienne was increasingly impressed with Miguel, a young and brilliantly creative writer with the agency. As a first-generation immigrant from Mexico and a gay man, Miguel was effeminate in his speech and gestures. Worried that Miguel's presentation would put off some of the agency's top clients—sports teams, traditional athletic brands, men's clothing—Adrienne often made ad pitches for Miguel, believing she was protecting him from disparagement and failure. Over time, however, Adrienne recognized that Miguel was not getting full credit for his creative ideas, and clients did not attribute their very successful ad campaigns to Miguel's work. Adrienne finally recognized that her own biases were undermining Miguel's career success.

Competent mentors demonstrate a low tolerance for blatant forms of bigotry, discrimination, and harassment. They reject behaviors such as racial slurs, unwanted sexual advancements, overt racism, homophobia, and bias in hiring and promotion. These acts have no place in a civil society, let alone a mentoring relationship. Psychologist Charles Ridley explains another type of bias. This bias is reflected in behavior that brings harm to people, but it is not the result of malicious intent. He explains the difference between *unintentional bias* and blatant, intentional bias. Many people who ordinarily reject blatant bigotry are unaware of their unintentional bias—their well-intended attitudes and behaviors that nevertheless harm people of marginalized groups.

Unintentional displays of bias, like intentional bias, channel access and opportunity to members of the advantaged group while simultaneously denying access and opportunity to members of the disadvantaged group. A senior male mentor seeks to protect his female mentee from the hardball politics within their organization. He has been around a long time and seen it all—turf wars and infighting, professional jealousy, cronyism, egos that are larger than life, and bosses who are promoted to their highest level of incompetence. Listen to the rationalizations in his head: "She might get discouraged and quit. What she really needs is to concentrate on her skill development so that she can become value added. Besides, she might misinterpret the politics as gender bias when it's just business as usual. We sure don't need another feminist around here making accusations of sexual harassment."

The mentor is right to be concerned about his mentee's growth and development. He also has a responsibility to protect her from unnecessary ruthless politics, the kind that serve no purpose in her development. However, his carte blanche dismissal of her need for exposure to any organizational politics is off point. Exposure to the realities of organizational politics should be an integral part of her professional development. The actions of the mentor deny her an opportunity for real-life exposure to challenge and stress likely to bolster her defenses and strengthen her immunity to attack. This is critical to her success and advancement.

Ridley warns that this type of bias is insidious. On the one hand, the mentor does not see the behavior as bias—just the opposite. The mentor believes wholeheartedly in the virtue of what he is doing, so much so that it will be hard to change his point of view. On the other hand, the consequences of the mentor's behavior are detrimental to the mentee. Instead of helping the mentee, he puts her in a disadvantaged position relative to her male peers. What they acquire that she does not is the acumen, astuteness, and confidence in navigating organizational politics.

The rule of thumb is that mentors have to judge the merits of their mentoring practice by looking at its consequences. This is not to say that they should disregard their good intentions. They simply need reminders that good intentions do not always result in good interventions. They always should structure developmental experiences that ultimately serve their mentees' best interests, even when this means exposure to uncomfortable or intimidating circumstances.

KEY COMPONENTS

- *Be mindful of the difference between intentional bias and unintentional bias.*
- *Remember that unintentional bias is insidious and can be as damaging, if not more so, than intentional bias.*
- *Carefully observe the outcomes of your mentoring behaviors with minority group mentees; be vigilant for unintentional consequences.*

Knowing Thyself as a Mentor

MATTERS OF INTEGRITY

We live in a culture of ambition and competitive productivity, but few of us are truly "up-to-date" on our own psychological, emotional, and spiritual status. Excellent mentoring demands self-awareness. Outstanding mentors are self-reflective; they frequently take time to become reacquainted with their own feelings, needs, wishes, and fears. The wise mentor understands the need for periodic reintroduction to the self. We call such self-awareness *mindfulness* and propose that mindfulness is a crucial ingredient of both effective and ethical functioning as a mentor.

Mindful mentors understand that they have imperfections, limitations, and weaknesses. They respect this side of their humanness in much the same way that they appreciate their talents, capacities, and strengths. They are honest about who they are as individuals, living by the maxim, "Know thyself." Because they are nondefensive and accustomed to thinking about their areas of vulnerability as well as their gifts, mindful mentors approach mentoring openly and as a challenging adventure. These mentors use their self-awareness to successfully navigate powerful yet delicate relationships with mentees.

Mindful mentors are also congruent. How they see themselves

is consistent with who they really are. They are not incongruent in the sense of allowing a gulf to exist between the "front" they present to mentees and their internal sense of self. Not surprisingly, such discrepancy leads to shame, denial, and self-blindness. In contrast, congruent mentors easily articulate thoughtful awareness of their own limitations: "You know, I'm aware of feeling unable to help you in this area. I feel uncomfortable giving you advice about something I don't know enough about myself." Congruent mentors say "I don't know" easily and without traces of shame or discomfort. Incongruent mentors, on the other hand, may attempt to feign knowledge, which may lead mentees astray and ultimately undermine the mentor's credibility.

In this section, we describe those elements of mentoring that pertain to knowing thyself—elements that require self-awareness and a realistic appreciation of the limits of one's competence. Mindful mentors actively consider the consequences of serving in the mentor role—both the benefits and the costs. They practice self-care. For instance, while investing heavily in their mentees, they take time regularly for personal rejuvenation. This may include routine physical exercise, time with family, and artistic or recreational pursuits. They also find creative ways to have periods without interruptions to minimize personal distress and stay productive. Then they intentionally model these strategies of personal and professional health. Not only do excellent mentors ensure their own competence in the mentor role, but they hold themselves accountable for their behavior as a mentor. Because mentoring generally is not a regulated activity, good mentors must be self-governing. Mindful mentors monitor their attitudes and feelings about their mentees, and they soberly appreciate the substantial power they wield over those they mentor. They are thoughtful about external perceptions of their mentorships and careful not to allow these to sabotage their mentees. Although mentors are often recipients of adulation and fawning praise from mentees, they must be practitioners of humility. Finally, excellent mentors are ever vigilant to avoid exploiting mentees. Of course, this requires acute awareness of their own desires and motivations. Mindful mentors temper personal ambition with an orientation toward service and the protection of their mentees.

53
Recognize the Costs of Mentoring

As an outstanding mentor, Jennifer was personally responsible for developing many of the company's star female executives. During her tenure as a senior vice president, she mentored many new female managers and acquired a reputation as the company's resident "star-maker." Although Jennifer had always been drawn to mentoring because of the satisfaction she derived from seeing her mentees grow and succeed, she became increasingly aware that her success in the mentor role also was beneficial for her own career. Not only did she receive strong praise and recognition from the CEO, her achievements in mentoring had been directly linked to several substantial bonuses over the years. On the other hand, Jennifer was acutely aware of how much time good mentoring required. Although rewarding, her mentoring efforts sometimes left her exhausted and behind on other projects. Jennifer responded to this self-awareness in three ways. First, she accepted her success in this arena while refusing to allow external rewards to become her primary motivation for mentoring. Second, she set limits on the number of people she committed to mentoring. Third, she was open with mentees about the various ways in which she benefited from being a mentor but also transparent about the costs linked to doing good mentoring work.

Mentoring is a responsibility not to be taken lightly. It entails many benefits, but many costs as well. First, let us consider the benefits. Although the research literature on mentoring highlights the rich benefits for mentees, mentors also stand to reap benefits. Tangible or extrinsic benefits may include reductions in workload, technical assistance, development of a loyal support base, recognition, financial rewards, and enhancement of one's own network. These benefits are not the primary motivators for most mentors. Many mentors savor the *intrinsic benefits* of mentoring. The most common intrinsic benefits are personal rejuvenation; excitement in working with a talented, energetic junior; and the satisfaction that comes from helping someone else succeed.

Second, let us consider the costs. Potentially the most insidious cost is the expenditure of time and energy. Other potential costs are high-visibility failures on the part of mentees (resulting in negative blowback on the mentor's reputation), sabotage or undermining by unscrupulous or disloyal mentees, and subtle innuendo or overt animosity from other professionals who feel threatened or jealous. Sometimes mentoring has costly repercussions for the mentor's personal life. For instance, a deep mentoring bond can reverberate into the mentor's marriage, creating confusion, discord, or jealousy. The time and effort put into mentoring can impinge on a mentor's social life, or it can take away valuable time from other responsibilities. In some situations, a mentor may lose perspective and become an institutional bully—all in the name of protecting a mentee. This obviously will erode credibility and later may be regretted. Then there is the finding that women and minority mentors tend to be closely scrutinized and, sometimes, penalized for mentoring. For instance, research reveals that when women mentor other women, they sometimes take a hit in their annual evaluations. But when men mentor women, they are praised as gender allies. The truth remains that women and minority-group mentors often live life under a microscope. When they—or their mentees—stumble, everyone seems to remember it.

Mentors need to appreciate the benefits and risks inherent in mentoring. Therefore, they should examine their motivations for mentoring. Awareness is a robust indicator of health and maturity in the mentor role. Many mentors are altruistic in that they have a strong sense of responsibility for serving and helping others develop. Yet they can delight in the experience of synergistic collaboration, and they may enjoy the accolades of peers and mentees regarding their mentoring acumen.

In rare instances, mentors harbor darker motivations. They may be motivated by power, control, or manipulation. They may regard mentees as objects to be used. They may be conflict avoiders or conflict producers. All of these tendencies may reflect their unresolved issues. For example, individuals with control issues simply may be acting out of a feeling of victimization or from a deep sense of powerlessness. These developmentally arrested and needy mentors are likely to be toxic for mentees—not just because of their problematic motivations for mentoring but also because of their lack of self-awareness.

KEY COMPONENTS
- *Recognize and accept the benefits of being a mentor, including extrinsic and intrinsic benefits.*
- *Recognize and accept the costs of being a mentor, including time and energy expenditures, potential for failure, and organizational scrutiny.*

- *Remain vigilant to consequences on one's relational life external to work.*
- *Increase awareness of your motivations to mentor—including self-serving motivations.*

54

Practice Self-Care

In his mentee Eric, Frank saw an earlier version of himself. A talented young researcher, Eric was a new addition to the university's biological research institute. On several occasions, Frank discovered that Eric had been in the lab all weekend or overnight. He cautioned Eric about overworking himself and neglecting his wife and infant child. Frank disclosed his own struggles with overwork and family neglect at times during his career and how this behavior had hurt more than it helped in the long run. More important, Frank shared how he learned to maintain clear boundaries (e.g., he went home at 5:00 p.m. each day regardless of how much work remained, and he refused to take on new projects when he determined that doing so would outstrip his staff's time and resources). Frank also spent each lunch hour jogging and always invited new staff to find some time during the day in which they would exercise. Over time, Eric came to appreciate his mentor's emphasis on self-care and integrated many of these habits into his own approach to life and work.

Mentors who fail to care for themselves may reach a point where they are unable to care for their mentees. Eager to succeed, some mentors unwisely disregard their own needs. But not even the greatest of mentors is Superman or Superwoman—just a capable human being. That is why mentors who endure over the long haul attend to their personal needs and consistently practice self-care. Let's face the facts: Mentoring is hard work. It requires time and resources beyond the normal work week. Mentors who fail to safeguard their physical and emotional health are setting themselves up to be of no benefit to themselves or their mentees.

On this subject, the research is clear about what mentees want from mentors. They want exemplars who can serve as models of how to balance their professional and personal lives. They want to see in action—not just in theory—how to set boundaries. In the back of the mind of every mentee is a nagging question: "Can I have a successful career and still have a satisfying personal life?" The mentee looks at the lifestyle of the mentor for an answer. Mentors can also help mentees who are seeking career advancement to say "no" to overwork without feeling like they're putting their career at risk or jeopardizing opportunities for advancement.

Perhaps in the area of self-care, more than in any other area, it is paramount that mentors "walk the talk" and not simply "talk the talk." Preaching health and self-care but working excessively, neglecting one's physical needs, or failing to nurture important personal relationships only broadcast hypocrisy to mentees. Although some mentees will reject the mentor's lifestyle, others unfortunately will follow the mentor's example. The pattern of self-neglect then passes from one generation to the next.

How then do mentors practice self-care? They say "no" to new responsibilities or "opportunities" that compromise their health or quality of work. They follow through with commitments to family, friends, and mentees and safeguard these relationships. As we said previously, they clarify their expectations and set boundaries with their mentees. In times of unusual need or high demand, mentors may make special requests to mentees or other colleagues (e.g., "I really need you to take more leadership on this new project," or, "It would help me if I could honestly share with you my concerns about the organization, but I would need you to keep that information confidential," or, "I'm feeling overwhelmed and burned out lately. I'm going to take a few days off this week to rest and care for myself").

KEY COMPONENTS

- *Care for mentees by first caring for yourself.*
- *Understand that mentees need a mentor who models a responsible balance between personal and professional life.*
- *Just say "no" to excessive demands at work.*
- *Follow through with commitments to family, friends, and mentees.*
- *Model self-care overtly by taking time off and limiting time devoted to work.*

55

Be Productive

Felicia's arrival as the newest faculty member in the university's history department was greeted with delight by many of the department's majors and graduate students. The students had grown weary of the department's reputation as a bastion of deadwood. This was a reference to the fact that most of this large department's tenured faculty members were not very productive. A couple of them occasionally published book reviews in second- or third-tier journals, or they sometimes made presentations at professional meetings. But for the most part, the faculty's research and scholarly activity was not exciting. As a result, applications from prospective doctoral students had dropped to all-time lows. Things changed quickly when Felicia arrived and immediately formed a research group among the students. This weekly group generated a great deal of student interest and quickly became a sort of mentoring team. Not only did Felicia share drafts of her most recent articles and chapters of a forthcoming book, she organized several joint projects with students and submitted these for presentations at conferences. In addition to her active scholarly writing, Felicia modeled professional engagement as vice president of a national historical society and associate editor of a major journal in the discipline. Felicia's productivity was infectious. Within a couple of years, the number of graduate applications spiked. Many of the applicants specified an interest in working directly with Felicia.

You can only lead a mentee where you yourself have traveled. And you will be a more effective guide when you have traveled there recently. Of course, the best mentors are frequent flyers. Effective mentors are engaged in the professional landscape they claim as their own. They are deeply involved in the work of their discipline and are frequently in contact with colleagues and collaborators. Outstanding mentors assume leadership roles in the field and are seen by peers as hard workers and innovators. Whether their product is a new business, innovative ideas, journal articles, or research findings, effective mentors produce and have rich experiences to share with their mentees.

There are many reasons why mentees are drawn to productive mentors. Productive mentors create excitement and possibility. They are enthusiastic, committed, and engaged. They trail a wake of innovative ideas, new projects, and career opportunities for mentees. Mentors on the cutting edge in any field create visibility and strategic access to resources and influence for mentees. In university settings, the most productive scholars bring substantial grant funding to their institutions—including full financial support for mentees. They also bring visibility and prestige to their institutions. In business, productive leaders are rewarded with more resources and enjoy greater allocation of perks. In addition, productive mentors are ultimately the best models. Because they are actively involved in the work of the profession, they offer a tangible example of how to carry out complex professional tasks. If a mentor is not active in the work of the profession, his or her effectiveness dissipates.

What about the unproductive professional? Lack of production in one's field is a red flag. Potential mentees may be advised to avoid this mentor altogether. Lack of productivity may signal one of three problems: (1) professional disengagement, (2) poor motivation, or (3) poor professional self-esteem. The disengaged mentor has become bitter or disenchanted with the profession. The unmotivated mentor sees no value in continuing to contribute or produce products in his or her field. The mentor with poor self-esteem feels insecure or unworthy—perhaps viewing oneself as incompetent and fearful of being revealed. Whatever the cause, unproductive people probably should not mentor. They cannot easily lead mentees where they have not traveled. Active and engaged productiveness is one hallmark of an ideal career mentor.

To ensure that they are performing at a level that affords them credibility for mentoring, mentors are advised to solicit feedback on their performance. For instance, an academic might honestly assess recent scholarly productivity, or a manager might participate in a 360 assessment. This is a comprehensive assessment that entails getting feedback on performance from superiors, peers, and subordinates.

KEY COMPONENTS

- *Be active in your field and productive as a professional.*
- *Remember that your mentee will benefit both directly and vi-*

cariously when you model engagement and leadership in your profession.

· Evaluate reasons for drops in your productivity and consider whether you are the best mentor for a potential mentee.

56

Resist Cloning

Mary's track record as a mentor was impeccable. As a senior Coast Guard officer and director of a competitive leadership program, she enjoyed the luxury of hand selecting high-flying junior Coast Guard officers. Her selections entered an intensive leadership program designed to groom these rising stars for promotion. Mary enjoyed mentoring several of the officers in each cohort who showed particular promise as future leaders. Gene was no exception. Unusually talented, self-confident, and interpersonally savvy, Gene had all the makings of a future admiral. Without realizing it, Mary began grooming him for a series of jobs that closely matched her own career trajectory and that would nicely position Gene for competitive promotions down the line. But the more she pushed, the more quiet and disengaged Gene became. Eventually, he confessed to having little interest in making the Coast Guard a career. Although he appreciated her efforts on his behalf, he envisioned leaving the service to work for a nonprofit environmental organization. Stunned, Mary reacted with a mix of anger and sullen withdrawal. It took some time and honest soul-searching for Mary to come to the realization that she had been trying to clone Gene in her own image.

Mentoring is one thing; cloning is another. Mentoring entails the development of mentees to maximize their potential. *Clon-*

ing entails the creation of mentees to be replicas of their mentors. Some of the activities involved in mentoring and cloning indeed are similar, and on the surface the two processes may appear indistinguishable. But below the surface there is a major distinction. Mentoring is mentee centered. Cloning is mentor centered.

Beware! Gratification and validation come with having talented mentees who want to be just like you. Sure, it is deeply satisfying to have subordinates who admire and respect you. Mentees interested in replicating your career trajectory are a stroke to your ego. But this can be dangerous. Unless you are careful, there is a downside—not unlike that faced by parents who try to realize their dreams through their children and expect their children to be just like them.

The research on mentoring bears this out. Mentors are most impressed with individuals who remind them of themselves. When mentors list their most successful mentees, they usually identify those who have taken strikingly similar career paths. When mentees take alternative career paths and make choices in life that are different from their mentors, the mentoring relationship dims. Whether or not you want to accept this reality, most of us tend to approve of, endorse, and stay connected to mentees who share our vocational interests, professional values, and career path.

The most dangerous aspect of cloning is not the process itself but the unconscious motivation underlying the behavior. When asked about promoting the careers of their mentees, most mentors give lip service to unconditional support. In practice, we see something else. Mentors advise, encourage, cajole, pressure, and sometimes even insist that mentees will be best served by following in their footsteps. The most egregious behavior stemming from unconscious motivation is coercion and abuse.

Cloning often plays out in subtle behaviors. Mentors may attempt to force their interpretation of reality on a mentee—unfairly diminishing the mentee's experience and perspective. The need to be correct or confirm one's own approach to meaning-making trumps any of the mentee's ideas that pose a challenge. This attitude of mentors is fertile ground for an abusive relationship. Such coercion is particularly dangerous when the mentee's cultural background or gender identity is dismissed in the process. Here is a rule of thumb: if your mentee's interpretation of events, perspectives, or career dreams causes you to become defensive, insecure, or angry, you may be overinvested in shaping your mentee into a junior version of yourself.

Mentors put mentees in a difficult bind when they pressure them to accept the mentors' personal points of view or make career choices that do not fit their personal goals. On the one hand, most mentees are loyal and crave acceptance. They stand by mentors and remain committed as a way of maintaining the emotional bond so central to good mentorship. On the other hand, their loyalty can become an unwanted burden. The pressure to conform to the mentor's expectations can conjure up feelings of resentment, ambivalence about the relationship, and guilt at the prospect of leaving or disappointing the mentor.

Resist cloning your mentees!

KEY COMPONENTS

- *Discover your mentees' dreams and aspirations and encourage these.*
- *Do not force mentees to conform to your personal ideal career path.*
- *Recognize that efforts to "clone" mentees are often subtle and insidious.*
- *Avoid exploiting mentees' loyalty by coercing them to conform to your values and beliefs.*

57

Make Sure You Are Competent

A newly minted PhD and a first-year professor in a large po-
litical science graduate program, Dr. Franklin was a strong
teacher and researcher. He was competent in the subject
matter in his courses and had a mature grasp of the academic/
professional landscape his graduate students would soon be
facing. Although adept in many regards, Dr. Franklin was
less comfortable interpersonally. Shy and introverted by na-
ture, he typically was reticent and awkward in interpersonal
situations—including informal exchanges with students. Aware
that mentoring required more than technical knowledge,
Dr. Franklin began working with a psychologist at the
university counseling center who was skilled in executive
coaching. After a few months of intensive interpersonal skill
development, he felt considerably more comfortable in struc-
turing and managing relationships with students. In order to
help safeguard his students while improving his interpersonal
acumen, Dr. Franklin asked a senior professor in the depart-
ment for occasional supervision (discussion and advice) related
to his various faculty-student mentorships. Finally, he was
upfront with students early on that some found him "quirky" at
times and asked his mentees to recognize that it was just his
personality style.

To be successful, mentors really need two types of competence.
They need to be competent in their professions, and they need
to be competent as mentors. Because there are no credential-
checking agencies or professional organizations that certify mentoring competence, it is incumbent then upon mentors to ensure
their own competence and fitness to mentor.

Mentor competence is rarely considered—let alone evaluated—during a professional's training. This holds true in business and in academic settings. Holding positional authority or supervisory status in an organization is often equated with competence to lead, supervise, and mentor. We know this is not always true. Some people who try their hand at mentoring lack the technical or relational capabilities required for success.

Prospective mentors should honestly consider whether they possess the requisite on-the-job experience, professional expertise, wisdom, and knowledge to truly be of benefit to a potential mentee. Because ethical guidelines in most fields prohibit professionals from practicing outside their area of competence or expertise, prospective mentors must engage in some self-analysis regarding competence or preparedness to effectively help another in a long-term developmental relationship. Mentors who are unsure of their own job performance experience role ambiguity. They are likely to receive lower motivation and performance ratings from mentees. Competent mentors must be experienced in the job at hand, confident and successful in their own right, and capable of safely and benignly managing relationships with mentees who remain largely vulnerable to the mentor's power throughout the course of the relationship.

Although some supervisors technically are competent career mentors—imbued with the requisite experience, professional confidence, and ethical-mindedness—they are inept in managing relationships. Competence to mentor demands that mentors exude benign personality characteristics as well as a good measure of interpersonal savvy. Listening skills, warmth, caring, and preferably a sense of humor are needed. Without relational expertise, even the most technically competent mentor will find it difficult to effectively deliver career guidance. The seeds of coaching, teaching, and guidance will wither if sown upon parched interpersonal soil.

A word about technical competence: Real mentoring competence is made up of more than the sum of many mentoring techniques. Although competence demands several focal skills (e.g., listening, challenging, encouraging), it is essential that the mentor also develops a knack or sense for knowing when to apply them in specific contexts with specific mentees for maximal effect. The competent mentor is able to discern when a mentee requires teaching and when to pause and simply offer emotional support. The competent mentor understands when a mentee requires collegial friendship and when direct confrontation will stimulate necessary growth. The bottom line is that competence is complex. It represents a rich and sometimes hard-earned mixture of natural aptitude, training, and experience in the mentor role.

KEY COMPONENTS

- *Work at developing your technical and relational mentoring skills.*
- *Evaluate your own experience, expertise, and confidence level before serving as a mentor.*
- *Understand that competent mentoring is more than the sum of its parts.*
- *Accurately select and deliver specific mentoring skills at important junctures to benefit your mentee.*

58

Hold Yourself Accountable

A seasoned supervisor at a large federal agency, George was well versed in the art of mentoring. As a mentor, he was skilled, dependable, and helpful to the junior managers he identified as most promising. His relationship with Tammy was typical of his approach to mentoring. Once George had identified Tammy as an especially excellent performer, and well matched with George's own interests and personality, he committed to helping her career. George set aside time for Tammy, always followed through when he promised to review her work or observe her in a meeting, and, most important, he always gave her very kind but direct and honest feedback. As a result, Tammy never doubted George's integrity or reliability. Unknown to Tammy, George also met every month or two with a good colleague from another agency to engage in peer supervision and support. In this context, George shared concerns and solicited advice about how to best serve his mentees.

All enduring relationships are based on trust. Trust is the fabric or glue that binds mentor and mentee together in a safe, productive, and committed relationship. Stemming from the German word *trost*, meaning "comfort," trust signifies a state of confidence and security in relation to a significant other. When a mentor's behavior is characterized by consistency, honesty, and integrity, trust can be established and maintained. The consistency applies to overt and covert forms of behavior.

Ensuring integrity and building trust happens when mentors intentionally hold themselves accountable. The accountability should occur on two levels—one with the mentee and one with at least one trusted colleague. Accountability with one's mentees involves a range of attitudes and commitments, including doing no harm, placing the mentee's developmental needs first, and honoring commitments—from the smallest (diligence in keeping appointments) to the largest (protecting mentees even at substantial personal cost). Accountability also entails certain behaviors, including clear communication, maintenance of confidentiality, setting and maintaining boundaries between personal and professional roles, and the delivery of honest and timely feedback—even when unpleasant.

Mentor accountability is incomplete without attention to maintaining at least one solid collegial relationship characterized by mutual self-disclosure surrounding one's mentorships. Within the safe scrutiny of a confidential peer relationship, a mentor can share any number of concerns. A mentor may discuss issues of his or her own competence, feelings about mentees, concerns about romantic attraction, blurring of professional and personal roles, and anything else that might arise in the context of mentoring. In long-term, complex, and emotionally intimate mentorships, mentors may occasionally experience anger, distress, self-doubt, guilt, and intense sexual or romantic attraction. When such thoughts and feelings are aired in the presence of a trusted and capable peer, mentors are able to regain perspective and resolve the problem.

What about the erosion of trust in a mentorship? There are infinite ways of losing a mentee's trust, but they generally fall into two categories. Overt or "red-letter" offenses easily erode trust. An example of an overt offense is when a mentor violates a mentee's confidence, steals a mentee's work, or becomes vindictive or exploitive. Covert violations of trust can be more insidious, emotionally confusing, and destructive to mentees than overt offenses. The subtle nature of these offenses makes them more difficult to identify, but their destructive consequences can loom large. Take the mentor who offers only marginal assistance in return for substantial mentee output or a mentor who is covertly seductive. In both of these instances, the mentee is undermined but has to second-guess the intentions of the mentor. In sum, be aware that mentee trust is hard to earn, easy to squander, and an utter necessity for effective mentoring.

KEY COMPONENTS
- *Ensure that your behavior is characterized by honesty, consistency, and integrity.*

- *Be accountable to mentees by honoring commitments.*
- *Be accountable to mentees by routinely conferring with at least one trusted colleague about your mentoring and your relationships.*
- *Avoid endangering mentee trust through dishonesty, incongruence, or exploitation.*

59
Respect the Power of Attraction

Angie began mentoring Steve during his first year of study in an internationally known music conservatory. A gifted and energetic young pianist, Steve was a delight to teach and coach. Steve was clearly enamored and awed by Angie, a rather famous pianist, and Angie found that she enjoyed Steve's devotion and fawning attention. Angie found Steve to be bright, talented, and quite attractive. She found collaborating with him interesting, exciting, and in some way renewing. As the year unfolded, Angie became increasingly aware of powerful feelings of attraction toward Steve. Angie's marriage was stale, and she began spending an increasing amount of time fantasizing about a romantic future with her mentee. Finally, aware that she was losing the ability to objectively and helpfully evaluate Steve's progress, Angie sought out a colleague at the conservatory and shared her dilemma about Steve. After some good consultation, she agreed it best to transition Steve to another faculty pianist. Although she accepted her human feelings of attraction and saw them as a not uncommon facet of a close mentorship, she simultaneously recognized the power differential in the relationship, the ethical difficulties involved in embarking on a relationship with a trainee, and the obvious risk to Steve of feeling coerced or exploited by his mentor. She remained supportive of Steve's career, introduced him to other master pianists, and limited her contact with him.

In close working relationships, developing interests that go beyond work is not uncommon. Attraction is a powerful force, and only naïve professionals deny this reality. Mentors sometimes experience intellectual, emotional, romantic, and sexual attraction to their mentees. Attraction often involves some combination of these elements. But attraction itself is not a problem. It is human. Denial and the mishandling of attraction are the real problems, for these responses get mentors into trouble.

Egregious and public problems linked to attraction and sexual feelings are the most common in mentorships in which the mentor is male and the mentee is female. This is partially a result of the large proportion of men at senior levels in many organizations and partially a function of the difficulty some men have maintaining wholesome friendships with women without sexualizing the relationship. Considering that mentorships are formed on the basis of shared interests and some degree of compatibility and that the relationship may extend over a long period of time, it is not surprising that the mentorship context, for both cross-gender and same-gender pairings, is fertile ground for developing intimacy. Attraction problems can range from strong sexual feelings to emotional dependency and exploitation. The attraction may be unidirectional—from mentor to mentee or from mentee to mentor. The attraction also may be reciprocal—both individuals are attracted to each other. Mentors are usually surprised by the full power of attraction and even more surprised when they find themselves in a compromised position. This is why they must manage their attraction in a responsible manner.

Few mentors receive training to help them handle attraction in professional relationships. Certainly, human resources provides regular training on employee protections and guidelines for reporting sexual harassment. However, training in handling attraction is fundamentally different from training in handling and reporting violations. The former is preventative, while the latter is remedial. The unavailability of training to handle attraction is also concerning because many mentees, especially women, report sexual contact with educators and supervisors. Even when there is no physical involvement, mentors may experience feelings of guilt, shame, anxiety, and confusion due to their emotional involvement. The worst cases are when mentors become physically involved with mentees but delude themselves that the relationship is merely collegial. They ignore the mentor–mentee power differential and fail to anticipate the long-term consequences of their involvement.

How then should mentors respond to the power of attraction? First, they must develop self-awareness. They should ask themselves these questions: "How often am I thinking about this person and in what way?" "Do I treat this mentee preferentially?" "Where do I hope this relationship may be headed?" "What emotional needs am I trying to meet in this mentorship?" Second, they must accept their humanness. Mentors can engage in constructive self-talk such as, "It makes good sense that I find this person attractive, we are well matched in many areas, and he or she is quite talented. Thank goodness I am human and can experience attraction. It is not a catastrophe." Third, they must get consultation. We mean the collegial accountability referred to in element 58. They must discuss the attraction and its roots and devise a plan for responding. Of course, discussing such attraction with the mentee is inadvisable, for it opens the door to seducing the mentee or creating unnecessary turmoil for the mentee.

In some mentorships, those that are well developed and characterized by a great deal of maturity on the part of both members, attraction can be discussed at various times as a way of ensuring accountability to professional boundaries. In most cases, however, it is the mentor's responsibility to carefully attend to evidence of growing attraction, consult with a colleague, and devise a plan either for continued mentoring or, in a few cases, termination of a mentorship that can no longer be professionally productive.

Can a mentorship ever become a deeper personal relationship without harming the mentee? In some circumstances, yes. Examples exist in business, academia, and other settings of the mentor–mentee pair who become apparently well-adjusted and happily married spouses. A problem with these exceptional cases is that they serve to distract from the vast majority of romanticized and sexualized mentorships that do not end happily. In most cases, the mentee feels exploited and simultaneously deprived of a long-term mentor.

Another problem is that these types of relationships violate ethical codes in some professions. For example, multiple relationships are unethical for psychologists. The ethical principle rests on the premise that romantically involved psychologists can no longer be objective about focusing on their client's best interests; romantic involvement compromises the quality of their professional service delivery. In the same manner, a supervisor who has sexual intimacies with an intern compromises the relationship, demonstrates impaired judgment, and most likely may not be able to provide an impartial evaluation of the intern's performance. Impairment in the supervisor's judgment can have negative consequences for the intern not only personally but also professionally.

KEY COMPONENTS

- *Accept attraction as a common and expected phenomenon in some well-matched mentorships.*

- *Maintain self-awareness regarding feelings of attraction toward mentees.*
- *Seek out collegial consultation when attraction threatens to undermine or negatively alter professional boundaries.*
- *With very few exceptions, do not disclose attraction to mentees.*
- *Remember that romantic involvement with a mentee constitutes a breach of professional boundaries.*

60

Address Public Perceptions

A vice president at a Wall Street financial company, Bob was troubled by a nagging realization. Although he was a prolific mentor for male up-and-comers in the company, most of the talented junior women he tried to initiate positive developmental relationships with never seemed to follow through and engage him as a mentor the way men did. It took a conversation with another vice president—a woman—to make the lightbulb go on for Bob. She observed that Bob seemed to conduct all of his mentoring after hours, often at bars for drinks or restaurants for dinner. She remarked that meeting after hours with a senior male might be uncomfortable for many junior women, owing to concerns about starting "sleeping her way to the top" rumors. Recognizing that his own practice was creating an uneven playing field for women, Bob quickly developed what he called his "breakfast or lunch only policy." Going forward, he stopped all after-hours meetings with junior employees and instead had his assistant schedule mentoring meetings only for breakfast or lunch at a café near the company. The effect of this new policy was dramatic. Within a year, he noted that he was mentoring nearly as many women as men. He wondered, "How could I have been so oblivious?"

When it comes to effective mentoring, here is an important rule: *don't give them something to talk about.*

Human beings love to talk. We seem wired to enjoy gossip, especially titillating rumors about potential romantic or sexual liaisons. It is incumbent upon mentors to be aware of how their mentoring relationships are perceived. In effect, there are always two relationships when you mentor another person. First, there is the *actual* relationship. This is the day-to-day interaction experienced by mentor and mentee in which the emphasis genuinely is focused on the growth and development of the mentee. Second, there is the *external* relationship, the interaction seen through the eyes of others in the organization. Unfortunately, the actual relationship and external relationship are not always consonant. As you might imagine, the greater the discrepancy between the actual and external relationship, the greater the risk that perceptions—whether fair or unfair—might harm the mentee or the mentor or undermine the relationship.

The most common public perceptions that threaten a mentorship are those in which the relationship has become unduly familiar, perhaps romantic, and possibly even sexual. These perceptions are fueled by unusually frequent meetings, spontaneous meetings, meetings outside of work hours or the workplace, use of overly familiar language or nicknames, physical touch, or even tone of voice and facial expressions. These behaviors broadcast to others in the organization that something about the relationship is too intimate to be purely professional. Of course, even if observations and rumors lack a sexual component, perceptions that a mentor picks favorites among mentees or is unduly friendly (e.g., drinking buddies) with a mentee can create a groundswell of animosity and resentment, particularly among the mentee's peers.

How can negative perceptions and a poorly managed external relationship harm your mentee? Let us count the risks. First, even when rumors and innuendo are baseless, they may become toxic. For instance, others may attribute a mentee's success to currying special favor with a senior person, his or her attractiveness, or a brazen willingness to use a sexual relationship to climb the ladder. Second, jealous coworkers and peers may deliberately fabricate false rumors about sexual intimacy to undermine the credibility of the "favored" mentee. The fabrication makes the mentee a lightning rod for intensified jealous hostility from others. Third, the career potential of the mentee is put into jeopardy.

And let's not forget, external perceptions can undermine a mentor too. When mentors are perceived as blurring boundaries with a mentee, becoming "buddies" with a supervisee, or, worse, possibly exploiting a mentee sexually or otherwise, their credibility quickly goes out the window. Paradoxically, the negative perceptions ultimately will undermine their ability to effectively promote a mentee. If others in the organization attribute a mentor's praise for a mentee to biased favoritism or romantic feelings, the affirmation is likely to be discounted. Last, keep in mind that perceptions of a "special" relationship with a mentee might also cause negative ripple effects in one's relationship with a partner or spouse. Sometimes, a jealous partner might be an indication that a mentorship has become unduly intimate.

So, what can a mentor do to minimize the probability that toxic rumors about a mentorship will torpedo its value for the mentee? Here are several recommendations: First, *be transparent*. Never hide a mentoring relationship from others. Be open and clear about who you are meeting with and whose career you are championing. Schedule meetings formally when possible (even meetings for coffee or lunch) and meet in public locations at or near work. Second, *do not be exclusive*. If you suddenly begin spending a lot of time with only one mentee—especially a mentee of the opposite sex—people will notice. And for good reason. Although you may mentor only one person at a time, be deliberate in your track record about mentoring both men and women. This will convey that you are inclusive. Third, *discuss perceptions openly with mentees* and be alert to any rumors or gossip. Then, take steps to change anything about the external relationship that may be creating false perceptions. Fourth, enlist the support of a *truth ally*. The ally is a reliable and trustworthy colleague. Ask this person to share with you any concerns he or she has about your mentoring relationships and the perceptions others have within the organization. Asking a colleague to support you as an ally might empower that individual who otherwise might opt to be silent for fear of your reactions. Finally, *check yourself*. If your ally, your spouse, or others raise concerns, take them seriously and consider the possibility that a mentorship has veered off the professional rails.

KEY COMPONENTS

- *Try to align your actual mentorship with the external mentorship, the one that others in the organization perceive.*
- *Remember that rumors of impropriety or romance in a mentorship will undermine the mentee, the mentor, and any benefit accruing from the mentorship.*
- *Be nondefensive and responsive to feedback from others about how a mentoring relationship is perceived; take corrective measures if needed.*
- *Be consistent and transparent about whom you mentor and when and where you meet.*

61

Accept the Burden of Power

When Peter reflected on his career as a faculty member of a medical residency and mentor to several generations of surgery residents, he often smiled and shook his head at some of his early career blunders. As a young and experientially green supervisor, Peter often had failed to appreciate the profound power he wielded vis-à-vis his residents. During those early years, Peter frequently blurred boundaries with residents (e.g., socializing, dating, developing close personal friendships) that tended to compromise the impact of his positional authority. In order to feel like "one of the gang," Peter minimized his role as supervisor and evaluator—often causing confusion among his residents. As Peter matured, he developed an increasingly sober appreciation for the tangible power he held in relation to those he supervised. His evaluations carried real weight in influencing a resident's ranking and subsequent job possibilities. Peter gradually realized that his denial of power actually undermined his credibility with residents. He became careful about boundaries with students and conscientious in the use of his positional power for the benefit of those he mentored.

Power is influence. In all mentorships, there is an implicit power differential between the mentor and mentee. The mentor is in the one-up position—particularly in the early phase of a mentorship—while the mentee is in the one-down position. Mentors can use their position of power for good, or they can abuse their power. Although mentors are conscious of the imbalance of power in most mentorships—particularly when the mentor owns a supervisory or evaluative role with a mentee—the master mentor ultimately endeavors to share power with mentees as an expression of career support and trust.

Wise mentors acknowledge that they wield substantial power. Seasoned and successful members of any organization or profession are the most influential and potent developers of junior personnel. This is the mentor's *reflective power*. The credibility, resources, and reputation of the mentor extend to the mentee; the mentee receives early credibility and entrée into important arenas of an organization precisely because he or she is associated with a powerful sponsor. Mentoring, by its very definition, signifies an unequal helping relationship focused primarily on the development of the mentee. This inherent power inequality makes mentoring a fiduciary relationship—a professional relationship in which partners are not on equal terms. The fiduciary party (mentor) must act with utmost good faith and primarily for the benefit of the dependent party (the mentee).

The mentor's power emanates from several sources. First, mentors often hold supervisory/evaluative authority over the mentee. Mentors may be key contributors to decisions about the mentee's ultimate success or failure. A mentor's endorsement will exert tremendous influence on whether the mentee will be competitive for subsequent jobs and promotions. Second, mentors are subject-matter experts; they wield the power of authoritative knowledge, experience, and wisdom. Third, mentors hold the psychological power. They give affirmation, nurturing, and endorsement. This source of the power differential holds the most potential impact because it is invisible and holds sway over the mentee's sense of well-being and belonging in the profession. It can feed into the imposter syndrome commonly experienced by neophyte mentees. Furthermore, the impact can endure long after the formal mentorship is over.

Some mentors misunderstand, underestimate, disregard, or have difficulty in accepting the power differential inherent in their role. Younger supervisors and those newest to their profession often have difficulty accepting the mantle of authority. Like the rebellious prince who refuses to assume duties as king, so the new mentor may work to deny or repress evidence of relative power vis-à-vis his mentees. Feeling insecure or fearful of possessing positional authority, this mentor hides from power and defaults to inappropriate peership with mentees. These actions compromise mentoring and confuse mentees. When parents or teachers shirk authority and attempt to join in with children, healthy kids rebel or reject them. When a mentor refuses to accept power and use authority constructively, the power of his or her position is inadvertently diminished.

Here is a last word. Although the power differential between you and your mentee may be more palpable and transparent early on, recognize that the best relationships become increasingly mutual, reciprocal, and collegial. They evolve from *power over* to *power with* relationships.

KEY COMPONENTS

- *Accept the power you may hold relative to your mentee.*
- *Recognize that your mentee benefits from your organizational power and credibility.*
- *Respect the power differential in the mentorship.*
- *Act solely for the benefit of your mentee.*
- *Use power to encourage, support, and bolster, but never to exploit.*

62

Model Humility

In nearly every way, General Frank Hastings was a model Marine Corps officer. A Naval Academy graduate, a combat veteran, and a very articulate and effective leader, General Hastings was well loved and respected by congressional leaders, peers, and subordinates. One of those subordinates, Major Greene, was General Hastings's aide and his primary mentee. One of the things that most amazed Major Greene about his mentor was the general's profound and apparently authentic humility and humanness. Although the general was very successful, he seemed to go out of his way to highlight his shortcomings, tell others about his mistakes, and laugh about his fallibility. Paradoxically, this habit further endeared the general to those around him. For example, whenever the major referred to the general's combat exploits or career successes, General Hastings would look him in the eye and say something like, "Major, I was in the right place at the right time. I'm a lucky man, and fortunate enough to be surrounded by brave and smart people—people like you." Although the general admitted that he was good at certain tasks and refused to engage in false displays of humility, he reveled in both accepting his limitations and modeling this acceptance to mentees.

Mentors who are self-aware, nondefensive, open to feedback, and humble in their self-assessments are highly preferred by mentees. One interesting line of mentoring research shows that mentors who underestimate the effectiveness of their leadership receive the highest quality-of-mentoring ratings from mentees.

Some level of sober, critical self-evaluation appears to be a prerequisite for outstanding role modeling. Transformational mentors are humble, modest, and conservative in their self-assessments. The humble mentor is perceived as approachable and real. In owning and even highlighting blemishes and imperfections, the mentor offers the mentee some real texture. At the same time, remember the wisdom of element 19: thoughtful mentors disclose primarily for the benefit of the mentee and are cautious about revealing too much. They draw the line by disclosing just enough personal information to show empathy and identify with the mentee but not too much whereby their disclosure is more about themselves than the mentee. "Perfect" mentors, or more accurately those who feign perfection, are distant, untouchable, and therefore unlikely to receive the mentee's authentic confessions of anxiety and struggle.

A defining feature of humility is an appreciation of one's limitations. The more accurate people are in their self-assessments, the more this is a reflection of humility. Humble people are not afraid to take an honest look at themselves—warts and all.

Effective mentors readily admit "I don't know" when this is true and are comfortable (versus enraged or mortified) when mentees see the limits of the mentor's expertise. They are not arrogant, self-absorbed, or narcissistic but reasonably self-confident and professionally poised. As we have already pointed out, excellent mentors are highly accomplished. So there is no contradiction between humility and competence. The key is that the humble mentor appreciates his or her assets as special gifts, not as evidence of personal grandeur. Mentors of this ilk focus less on self-centered outcomes and more on the developmental needs of mentees.

A humble mentor can model humanness and imperfection without shame or distress. Because he or she does not demand adulation from subordinates, the humble mentor is more available for mutuality and collegiality—the benefits of a real relationship. When humility is absent, the relationship is superficial and characterized by grandiose unreality. Further, the mentor may be intolerant of a mentee who elects a career path that diverges from that followed by the mentor. Finally, the mentor may be threatened and subsequently disparaging and rejecting of the mentee who is not satisfied to be cloned in the image of the mentor.

KEY COMPONENTS

- *Practice humility through nondefensiveness and transparency with respect to faults and weaknesses.*
- *Understand that by authentically admitting limitations, you give your mentee permission to be human as well.*
- *Acclimate yourself to the idea of admitting mistakes and saying "I don't know."*
- *Appreciate your own strengths and accomplishments while using them to promote your mentee, not gratify yourself.*

63

Never Exploit Mentees

As the only female in senior management for a large IT firm, Eun often felt that she lived her work life in a fishbowl or under a microscope. Everyone seemed to be watching—skeptically she often thought—to see whether a woman really belonged. To make matters worse, her vice president seemed to be testing her by assigning an inordinate workload. Don was one of Eun's junior managers and, in her view, a rising star in the company. She appreciated Don's talent and tenacity and

*began turning to him often to help her manage her own work-
load. Eun framed their relationship as mentoring, and, indeed, she did occasionally pass along career advice to Don. Yet
over several months, Eun noticed that her mentoring conversations with Don dropped off as she became busier, more
stressed, and asked Don for more and more assistance with her
own work assignments. Don began to look fatigued. Eventually, Eun faced the truth that she was exploiting Don and his
willingness to be helpful. Don was carrying an exorbitant
amount of work and receiving mediocre mentorship in return.
Eun immediately apologized to Don and began limiting their
joint work projects to things likely to be career-enhancing for
Don while spending more time providing him with intentional career and personal support.*

Exploitation is the selfish use of someone else for one's own ends
or profit. It translates into treating people as objects rather than
as human beings. Exploitation also involves taking an unfair
advantage. A person in a position of relative power and authority exploits a person who is in a power-down, dependent, or
vulnerable position. Although most mentors are repelled by the
notion of exploiting a mentee and thereby sullying an inherently
trusting and benevolent relationship, evidence suggests that mentees are frequently exploited in a variety of ways.

Surveys of graduate students, junior managers, and other employees find an alarming number of women who report sexual
harassment or sexual contact with male mentors. As time elapses
from the actual occurrence of these experiences, these mentees
increasingly report feeling exploited and negatively impacted.
Although mentors (male or female) often perceive mentees as
mature colleagues, conscientious mentors acknowledge to themselves their ever-looming potential to be exploitative.

Sexual exploitation is unmistakably a bright-line offense that most mentors clearly recognize and guard against. But many other forms of exploitation exist. Some are more subtle than sexual exploitation. However, these too can have harmful consequences. The most common of these include emotional and professional exploitation. *Emotional exploitation* occurs when the mentor (often unaware) attempts to use the mentorship—and the mentee—to satisfy unmet and often powerful emotional needs. Requiring the mentee to listen at length to personal complaints and dissatisfactions or satisfy needs for nurturing, or demanding adulation and fawning allegiance from mentees can be exploitive.

Professional exploitation may occur when a mentor takes unfair advantage of the mentee's work or professional products. When a manager or professor presents a mentee's work as entirely (or even primarily) his or her own, the mentor is exploiting the mentee. In other cases, a mentor may demand exceptional productivity and devotion to long work hours without ever legitimizing the mentorship through commensurate coaching, sponsorship, or support. This relationship is exploitive simply because it benefits the mentor exclusively.

Subtle forms of exploitation are not always easy to detect. However, they usually are preventable. What mentors must keep at the forefront of their thinking is how their mentees benefit from the expectations, assignments, and demands placed on them. If benefits can be identified, more than likely the chances of exploitation are reduced. If benefits to the mentee cannot be identified, the chances of exploitation are greatly increased. An important question for mentors to ask themselves is this: "How do I benefit from this expectation versus how does my mentee benefit?" By intentionally keeping the focus of the mentorship on the mentee's growth and development and by accepting their inherent power in relation to mentees, mentors reduce the probability that a mentorship will become exploitive.

KEY COMPONENTS

- *Refuse to take unfair advantage of mentees.*
- *Recognize that mentees are usually vulnerable to some extent and can easily become the victims of exploitation.*
- *Be aware of both overt (e.g., sexual) and subtle (e.g., emotional, professional) temptations to exploit.*

64

Balance Advocacy with Gatekeeping

As a federal court judge, Armando enjoyed working with law clerks from some of the nation's top law programs. Every year or two, an especially talented clerk would come to Armando's attention, and an informal mentorship would commence. Armando had a reputation for shepherding these clerks into prime jobs after graduation. He often would become a powerful advocate and lobbyist on behalf of his mentees. His relationship with Jacob, a talented law student and motivated clerk, was no different. Armando began to spend more time with Jacob, grooming him for eventual employment in the profession. But things began to unravel when Jacob was accused of plagiarism by a law school professor and Armando subsequently was informed that Jacob had falsified several pieces of information in his clerk application. Other suspicious behaviors ensued, giving Armando cause to doubt Jacob's integrity. Although he was fond of Jacob, Armando's hand was forced. With deep regret, he found he no longer could stand behind Jacob and advocate for his advancement in the legal profession. To do so would

compromise his own integrity as well as his sense of obligation
to the public and the profession.

Advocacy is a common practice in personal and professional affairs. Advocates speak on behalf of or argue for someone else, typically a person who is in a less powerful position. Although the importance of advocacy may go unacknowledged, it is vital to effective mentoring relationships. By championing their cause, mentors do for their mentees what mentees cannot do for themselves—open new doors and create opportunities for advancement. But blind advocacy is unwise. It can lead to a host of counterproductive outcomes for mentees, organizations, and mentors themselves. Wise mentors advocate with their eyes wide open. Before they speak on behalf of their mentees, mentors make it their business to know their mentees' characters and competences. And they determine when it is right to champion them and when it is right to withdraw their support. In some rare instances, the only right course of action is to advise a mentee to leave the profession.

In the literature on mentoring, satisfied mentees describe their mentors as protective and supportive advocates. The metaphor of a shepherd is relevant here. Good mentors guide their mentees through vulnerable career stages and personal transitions. As the mentorship unfolds, the relationship often becomes less hierarchical, more collaborative, and more personally transforming. In many cases, a significant friendship emerges. No wonder mentors often evolve into stalwart and partisan advocates for mentees.

But professionals in most disciplines also are obligated by ethical guidelines, organizational policies, and even legal statutes to render honest evaluations of those they supervise. When a mentor is also a supervisor or when a mentor's recommendation will influence whether a mentee gains entrée into a profession, the mentor holds an ethical and moral obligation to fairly and accurately assess the mentee's performance and aptitude. When a mentor downplays evidence of a mentee's incompetence, flaws in character, or insensitivity to ethics and instead advocates stridently on the mentee's behalf, the mentor actually is complicit when the mentee later inflicts harm on consumers, wreaks havoc in an organization, or tarnishes the reputation of an institution or profession.

Why are mentors vulnerable to blind advocacy? There are several reasons. First, the temperament of some mentors predisposes them. Mentoring scholar Tammy Allen discovered that excellent mentors are often high on measures of empathy and tendency to care for others. Possessing a need to be helpful and empathetic, some mentors mistakenly may see others—especially their mentees—through rose-colored glasses. They may minimize evidence of impairment or incompetence and focus exclusively on potential. Second, some mentors fail to take stock of their evolving emotional connection to mentees. As a mentorship moves along a mentoring relationship continuum, becoming increasingly familiar and connected, mentors may become more partisan in their attitudes. Their dogged advocacy for mentees might be devoid of objectivity. Third, mentors may ignore the fact that not every mentee will have the requisite qualities and temperament to succeed in the mentor's field. Worse, some may harbor grandiose fantasies that stellar mentoring will offset these essential deficits. Finally, some mentors may feel ashamed at the prospect of a mentee's failure. They engage in denial, even when confronted with clear evidence of a mentee's incompetence.

Balancing advocacy with gatekeeping is fundamental to the integrity of the mentor. Seasoned mentors accept the pervasive tension between wholehearted support for mentees and the ethical and moral imperative to render timely, honest, and objective evaluations of mentees' character and competence. Here are some strategies for successfully navigating this dilemma:

1. Recognize that you may become increasingly fond of mentees and subsequently more inclined to downplay shortcomings and magnify strengths in your evaluations and recommendations—no mentor is immune to this type of bias.
2. Make routine and objective assessment and feedback a key component of the mentorship.
3. Maintain enough professionalism in the relationship so that providing corrective feedback is not uncomfortable.
4. Accept that not every trainee or mentee ultimately will be cut out for the profession.
5. Recognize that encouraging a mentee to leave an academic program, apprenticeship, or profession may be the most humane and responsible course of action.

Accept the fact that you may become an increasingly partisan promoter of your mentees while working diligently to focus on objective markers of competence and performance. If recommending a mentee for any opportunity makes you uncomfortable, honestly evaluate the reasons why and soberly consider your obligations to protect the public and the profession.

KEY COMPONENTS
- *Recognize the tendency to become a biased advocate for mentees.*
- *Balance obligations to mentees, the public, and the profession.*
- *Tell the truth in letters of recommendation and other promotional efforts.*

- *Make constructive appraisals a routine element of each mentorship.*
- *Accept that not every mentee will be a good fit within your profession.*

. . .

When Things Go Wrong

MATTERS OF RESTORATION

Mentorships are special relationships. Nothing compares to the dynamics that exist between a mentor and mentee. But mentorships are similar to other relationships in one important respect: they are imperfect and subject to human foibles. Some mentorships become riddled by conflict or dissatisfaction, or they result in disturbing endings. Some become downright unhealthy, dysfunctional, or, sadly, emotionally destructive. This is the dark side of mentoring—the side that some mentors find difficult to face.

All mentors should be open to the possibility that things can go wrong. Due to their imperfections and those of their mentees, mentors need to be alert to signs that might undermine their relationships. It's crucial to address problems as quickly as possible, judiciously, and in an attempt to restore the relationship. As seasoned mentors, we know from personal experience the heartache and disappointment of a mentorship gone wrong. We also know from experience how challenging it is to address these situations. The lessons we learned make us sensitive to the many mentors who unexpectedly one day will have to deal with disturbance in their mentorships.

How do mentors know when their relationships are in trouble? Among the many warning signs, three stand out as prominent:

1. The mentee or mentor does not believe some of their important developmental or professional needs are being met.
2. The mentee or mentor senses that the costs of the relationship outweigh the benefits.
3. The mentee or mentor feels distressed or harmed by the relationship.

A substantial body of research reports on the difficulties that may arise between a mentee and mentor. Either party or both parties may feel disenchanted, upset, or that they have been harmed by the other. Among the major contributing factors to these difficulties are poor matching between mentor and mentee (i.e., dissimilar backgrounds, interests, personality style), faulty communication, incongruent expectations, role conflicts (e.g., evaluative/supervisory versus helping roles), exploitation, abandonment or neglect, mentor incompetence (technically or relationally), boundary violations, problematic attraction, and unresolved disputes.

Using their common sense, competent mentors accept the reality of their own imperfections and those of their mentees. Then, with diligence and a sense of urgency, they unveil their competence by addressing any signs of relational distress and dissatisfaction. In this section, we discuss several key elements for handling mentorship difficulties. Our focus is on restoration. Regrettably, some mentorships cannot be restored, or they reach a point where a continuing relationship no longer serves the mentee's best interest. In further display of competence, mentors take the lead to end these types of relationships. In our view, however, this should be the action of last resort. Prior to reaching the point of no return, competent mentors make an earnest effort at restoration, though keenly aware that this is not always possible.

65
Above All, Do No Harm

Although the mentorship between Glen, a senior editor at a New York publisher, and Rick, a junior editorial assistant at the firm, began normally and was initially quite helpful to Rick and enjoyable to Glen, things took a turn for the worse when personality differences began to surface. Aggressive and ambitious by nature, Glen was a certified "workaholic." He frequently worked 70-hour weeks, was highly attuned to the power dynamics at the firm, and worked hard to compete against other editors for resources and prestigious projects. Although Glen expected the same of his mentees, he soon realized that Rick tended toward cooperation versus competition and favored more moderate work hours. Rick was competent and appeared to enjoy his work, but obviously he was disinterested in "beating out" his peers for promotions. An experienced mentor, Glen noticed himself becoming increasingly short-tempered and even disgusted with Rick's low-key and noncompetitive style. After some self-reflection, Glen realized he was most helpful to mentees who, like him, were driven, ambitious, and willing to "fight" their way to the top. Aware that these personality differences and his own low frustration tolerance were beginning to interfere with the mentorship and place Rick at risk for receiving unhelpful criticism based upon personality styles that were unlikely to change, Glen openly discussed the

> *problem of match with Rick and worked to find a better-suited editor with whom Rick could begin working. To his credit, Glen was careful to protect Rick from negative career outcomes and from feeling abandoned in the process.*

Mentors may not be able to fix every problem in their mentorships. Some problems are just too big, deep, or serious to handle. As much as possible, though, they can minimize the damage. The medical profession understands the importance of damage control. Physicians all over the world swear by the Hippocratic Oath, which begins with a sage warning: "First, do no harm."

Avoiding harm is called *nonmaleficence*. It is the most fundamental ethical obligation mentors have to their mentees. Nonmaleficence may also be the most difficult ethical obligation to uphold. A souring mentorship can get extremely complicated, befuddling even the most astute mentor. There are numerous ways to harm a mentee, either deliberately or unintentionally. Obviously, a mentor's harm can be blatant. An angry tirade, bitter criticism, or chronic disparagement laced with profanity will take a toll on even the most resilient mentee. More commonly, a mentor's harm is insidious. The behavior is not as easily identifiable as harmful, but the consequences are nevertheless real. Neglecting and ignoring mentees, tasking them with challenges for which they are ill prepared, sacrificing them on the altar of organizational politics, or forcing them to relinquish their creativity and individuality will undermine even the savviest mentee.

How do mentors avoid harm? We offer four major guidelines. First, as the primary power holder in the mentorship, mentors own the responsibility for ensuring that the mentorship benefits (versus harms) the mentee. They do not lay that responsibility on the shoulders of the mentee. Every deliberate effort they make to benefit the mentee counters any harm. Second, mentors set a priority on the professional and developmental needs of the mentee. Certainly, mentors do not deny their own needs. They simply do not allow mentoring to become "win-lose"—the mentor winning and the mentee losing. Third, mentors always treat mentees with dignity, respect, and compassion even when mentees are disappointing. Because mentors are human and have a vested interest in the mentee, they should guard against unwittingly resorting to behaviors that are unbecoming of a professional. If a mentor becomes personally impacted or outraged such that respect gives way to disrespect, the mentor more than likely should stop mentoring. Finally, mentors stay committed to the mentee but accountable to the organization. They serve the mentee's best interests, and they remain loyal and truthful to them. At the same time, they uphold obligations imposed by the sponsoring organization or profession. For example, a manager in an assigned mentorship would work to provide objective evaluations of a mentee and perhaps arrange for a smooth transfer when it becomes clear that the relationship is either unhelpful or destructive.

KEY COMPONENTS

- *Avoid harming your mentee either overtly or subtly.*
- *Take responsibility for ensuring that the mentorship benefits the mentee.*
- *Place your mentee's developmental needs before your own.*
- *Treat mentees with dignity, respect, and compassion—even when they disappoint you.*
- *Protect your mentee while honoring obligations to the organization and profession.*

66

Slow Down the Process

When June began working for a large commercial real-estate firm, she was impressed by Kathy, an experienced agent and manager. During June's first year in the firm, she looked for opportunities to work closely with Kathy and was delighted when Kathy began offering her career advice and involving June as an assistant in various managerial tasks. Things went smoothly until Kathy discovered that June had been gossiping about her to others in the firm—suggesting that Kathy was a "dinosaur" and that Kathy's business techniques were archaic and unnecessarily costly. Enraged, Kathy regretted the time she had invested in June, and she had an impulse to both confront June angrily and sabotage her career. Instead, she took several days to "cool off," collect firsthand accounts from other managers, and carefully prepare for a discussion with June. Through this decelerated process, Kathy discovered that the initial reports of June's behavior were exaggerated. She was able to calmly and clearly express disappointment to June and request that any further concerns be addressed directly to her. Although this event marked an inevitable muting of the relationship and the intensity of the pair's connection, Kathy's ability to control her impulse prevented a permanent fracture in the relationship.

When things go wrong, the events that take place can feel like they are on fast-forward. Dominos of emotion and reaction cascade right in front of you. Before you realize what is really taking place, problems in the mentorship escalate, unanticipated and deep emotions surface, and both parties begin to question how they ever got into the situation in the first place. In this atmosphere of turbulence, mentors cannot afford to have knee-jerk reactions or brush the problems aside. Neither is acceptable. Before they do anything, mentors should deliberately engage in thoughtful reflection, analysis, and consultation.

When mentors have quick and thoughtless responses to conflict or dysfunctional mentee behavior, the reactions may worsen the already tenuous situation. When mentors avoid addressing difficulties with mentees, these reactions also may exacerbate conflict and ultimately ensure the demise of the mentorship. Dysfunctional mentor behavior commonly appears in the form of self-defeating provocation or self-defeating passivity. The provocative mentor swiftly vents anger and frustration in a highly emotional and accusing manner—typically ensuring that the mentee responds in kind or emotionally withdraws from the mentorship. Furthermore, some mentors become active saboteurs; they betray the mentee or seek to harm them professionally as a means of exacting revenge.

The passively self-defeating mentor may engage in one of three unhelpful responses in the face of negative emotion or conflict. These include paralysis (the mentor freezes and fails to respond at all), distancing (the mentor intentionally disengages from the relationship and avoids the mentee altogether), and appeasement (the mentor passively capitulates, giving the mentee whatever he or she demands in hopes of diffusing conflict and restoring equilibrium). Each of these provocative and passive reactions is ultimately destined to worsen mentorship dysfunction, and none offer the mentee an adaptive example of professional conflict management.

Instead of responding impulsively or avoiding problems altogether, effective mentors engage in a deliberate process of analysis, reflection, and, when needed, consultation. They begin by listening carefully to the mentee's concerns or exploring the source of their own dissatisfaction or anger. They then consider their obligations to the mentee (e.g., do no harm, serve the mentee's best interests) and whether any ethical or professional standards have a bearing on the situation. Most important, mentors use this self-reflection to honestly evaluate their own contribution to the dysfunction. They can ask themselves how their behavior might have shaped the current state of affairs. When the causes of mentorship disturbance are clarified and the best interests of the mentee considered, the mentor explores possible solutions. In the exploration, mentors weigh the potential consequences of each solution. Ultimately, they decide on a course of action intended to have a dual benefit: the growth and development of the mentee and the resolution of the relationship disturbance.

KEY COMPONENTS
- *Take time to cool off and reflect before responding to problems or conflict with a mentee.*
- *Avoid provoking your mentee through angry outbursts or acts of revenge.*
- *Refuse to use passive strategies (paralysis, distancing, and appeasement) in the face of conflict.*
- *Examine the sources of dysfunction, including your contribution(s).*
- *Seek solutions that serve your mentee's best interests.*

67
Tell the Truth

When Kathleen, a professor of psychology, admitted Chris to a very competitive research-oriented doctoral program, she had high hopes that Chris would excel in his studies and go on to become a faculty member at a prestigious university. Over time, however, Kathleen found Chris to be only moderately motivated and prone to mediocre work. As Chris's mentor, Kathleen was approached by other faculty about Chris's substandard performance in their courses. Further, Chris was frequently late with assignments and neglected important research tasks in Kathleen's lab. Although Kathleen mentioned these concerns to Chris and attempted to help him develop very specific short-term goals and study habits, he continued to perform poorly. At the end of Chris's second year of study, Kathleen arranged a formal meeting and discussed Chris's well-documented shortcomings as a student. She was careful to emphasize her positive regard for Chris and to highlight his relative strengths. Nonetheless, Kathleen informed Chris that she could not continue to support him. Initially shocked, Chris admitted his ambivalence about graduate school and expressed appreciation for Kathleen's support and honesty.

The importance of telling the truth should be obvious—to make things better. When things go wrong with a mentee, however, a mentor can always make things worse. The mentor could decide to not discuss the problem, address it superficially, or be untruthful. All of these tactics are really forms of avoidance. To the contrary, a mentor always should try to make things better by approaching the problem head-on.

Just as mentors must take the lead in clarifying expectations with the mentee early in the relationship, they must take responsibility for alerting the mentee to early signs of relationship and performance problems. This is to prevent bigger problems later. The alert should be direct and constructive. When mentors avoid communicating concerns or frustrations to their mentees, they harbor a hidden agenda—one that is likely to reemerge in the form of neglect or hostility. When mentors opt to communicate concerns about the mentee through subtle innuendo or nonverbal cues, they actually are acting as an enabler of a dysfunctional and stagnant mentorship.

Some mentors find it difficult to be honest, especially when the honesty concerns delivery of unfavorable feedback. In fact, some deeply caring and technically competent mentors are chronically dishonest in this regard. They withhold critical feedback—information that is often essential for growth, change, and long-term success. Whether phobic about confrontation, fearful of hurting feelings, or anxious about rejection, these mentors fail at truth-telling and do a profound disservice to their mentees. Inadvertently, they perpetuate mentees' self-defeating or below-expectation performance behavior.

Experience suggests and research confirms that when a mentor–mentee pair experience conflict, resentment, or dissatisfaction, the relationship is most likely to be restored and strengthened when the mentor expresses concerns about the problem. To be successful, the mentor must typically plan to meet with the mentee for an open and honest discussion. If confrontation is required, the mentor must remain both kind and concrete. Even when confronting a mentee for significant errors, performance difficulties, or disloyal behavior, the mentor takes this high road. The wise mentor balances confrontation with compassion. As a matter of strategy, mentors typically begin a confrontational meeting with some reflection on the mentee's strengths and assets. Then they launch into the problem areas. This approach helps mentors convey a balanced picture of the mentee. It also helps to prevent an already difficult conversation from becoming unnecessarily difficult.

KEY COMPONENTS
- *Do not withhold honest and constructive feedback.*
- *Raise relationship or performance concerns immediately so they can be contained and addressed.*

- *Be direct and forthright when confronting problems, recognizing that passivity and innuendo are destructive.*
- *Plan feedback sessions carefully, and always begin with the positive aspects of the mentee's personhood and performance.*

68

Seek Consultation

A full professor and seasoned medical school faculty member, Audrey was delighted when a promising postdoctoral fellow, Larry, applied for a two-year fellowship under her supervision. Once selected, Larry began working on several of Audrey's grant-funded studies investigating the efficacy of a new medication for the prevention of dementia in older adults. Interpersonally savvy and intellectually bright, Larry struck Audrey as the ideal collaborator during the first several months of the fellowship. However, Audrey soon began to register concerns. Specifically, the data from one of her high-profile studies appeared too good to be true. Audrey had never seen such statistically significant results. The medication under study appeared to be a "wonder drug." When Audrey audited the data carefully, she discovered that Larry had deliberately dropped many dementia-positive subjects from the study. When she asked him about this, Larry winked and offered a flimsy rationale, noting that the drug's success would certainly lead to media attention and future grant funding for Audrey. Stunned, Audrey turned to her most reliable colleague at a different university and discussed the most appropriate way forward in addressing Larry's behavior, including her obligations to him as a supervisor and mentor. This consultation shored up her resolve. Following a difficult conversation in which Audrey confronted his unethical behavior, Larry was placed on probationary status, removed from a direct role in her research, and required to undergo ethics retraining. Through it all, Audrey remained firm but supportive, sensing that Larry's transgressions had more to do with inexperience and enthusiasm than any real character shortcoming.

No one can be expected to have the solutions to every problem. Sometimes mentors themselves need help, especially when they are dealing with complex ethical issues or vexing personal reactions. Under normal circumstances, ethical decision-making can be complicated. In mentorships that begin to go wrong, mentors can feel overwhelmed. They have to contend with their own biases and perceptions, strong emotions, or confusion regarding the best interests of the mentee. Examples of overwhelming situations are plentiful: a mentor has been consistently disappointed by a mentee and wonders about a mentee's ability to succeed in the profession; a mentee demonstrates sociopathic tendencies, questionable attitudes, or unethical behaviors; a mentor is strongly attracted to a mentee and on the verge of romanticizing or sexualizing a mentorship. Sorting out an appropriate and ethical response in each of these situations is difficult.

Mentors who seek out consultation from trusted colleagues are likely to make better decisions than those who do not. They are more inclined to proceed ethically and professionally in a troubling or challenging mentorship. In seeking out a consultant, mentors should look for a seasoned colleague known for a strong commitment to the profession, sensitivity to ethical matters, and a reputation for being both forthright and discrete. The last quality is important in safeguarding confidentiality in mentorships. Your success as a mentor will hinge on your reputation for protecting the privacy and confidences of your mentees. Therefore, exercise discretion regarding who you consult. Also, protect the anonymity of the mentee when this is warranted. One safeguard is to select a consultant in a different organization or distant geographic location. In smaller organizations, this may be the only way to really protect mentee confidence. Also, your own mentor may be the perfect confidant. Do not rule out your mentor even though the two of you are in the same organization. A trusted mentor may be ideally suited to understanding mentorship dynamics and care for you in the process of advice-giving. In this way, a mentor's legacy may be extended to more distant generations of mentees.

One other source of consultation might be beneficial: a former mentee who has become a colleague. Take your authors' own relationship as a case in point. Chuck Ridley has consulted with Brad Johnson regarding a knotty ethical matter. In his former role as chair of the Ethics Committee of the American Psychological Association, Brad was ideally suited to provide his wisdom and insights to bear upon Chuck's ethical concern. Incidentally, this illustrates the element of accepting friendship and mutuality in mentorship (element 20). Chuck and Brad's collegial bond has lasted over many years.

Excellent mentors use occasional consultation to develop a balanced and reasonable strategy for confronting mentees, handling ethical or legal issues, or developing clearer insight about a confusing relational dynamic. Consultation is particularly important if a mentor feels threatened or overwhelmed at the prospect of confronting a mentee or if the mentor has acted inappropriately and requires assistance in formulating a professional approach to restore the relationship. Finally, we cannot overemphasize the importance of using good peer consultation to explore one's own contributions to difficulties with mentees. Emotional problems (e.g., impulsive anger, neediness), personality traits (e.g., rigidity, narcissism), or management difficulties (e.g., becoming overextended and unable to attend to mentees) all contribute to mentorship problems. Good mentors use self-reflection and consultation to understand and modify these characteristics.

KEY COMPONENTS

- *Seek consultation from a trusted colleague when a mentorship has become complicated, concerning, or conflicted.*
- *Select a seasoned colleague with good judgment, ethical commitment, and a track record of discretion.*
- *Protect your mentee's privacy and identity by masking identifying information.*
- *Use consultation to formulate a mentee-oriented response.*
- *Explore your own contributions to difficulties with mentees.*

69
Document Carefully

As vice president for operations at a large manufacturing company, Clark was an effective mentor to several junior managers. Tom, a new mid-level manager in the company, came to Clark's attention. He was ambitious, hard-charging, and eager to respond to Clark's advice and attention. As a mentorship developed, Clark began a small file containing notes on Tom's achievements and projects. He also noted important exchanges between the two of them and recommendations he had offered. Maintaining a file was standard practice for Clark, who found these records very useful when writing future letters of recommendation for his mentees. During Tom's third month on the job, some red flags began to appear. Several supervising managers noted that Tom had a tendency to be abrasive, arrogant, and demanding—certainly not the type of behavior you expect of a junior manager, especially someone who is unproven. He became enraged when anyone questioned his decisions and sullen if another manager was singled out for praise. When Clark brought these concerns to his mentee's attention, he was met with angry accusations that he was "just like the others." Clark carefully documented these exchanges along with comments and complaints from other managers. Two months later, Tom was passed over for a promotion. Reacting with his customary rage, he accused Clark of "sabotage" and decided to file a suit against the company. Although he was shaken by this drama, Clark's detailed documentation of his attempts to mentor Tom proved essential in successfully defending the company.

You never know when documentation will come in handy. At the most unexpected time, it might save you a lot of grief and misunderstanding. It might avert a disaster.

Clear documentation of one's rationale and approach to responding to mentorship dysfunction—particularly when the relationship has thoroughly unraveled—is often the best defense against rare instances of vindictive mentee behavior or inaccurate accusations.

In very rare circumstances, a mentorship may fall apart. Although there are many potential sources of mentorship conflict, the most common—discussed at the outset of this section—include faulty communication, neglect of a mentee, unresolved disagreements, perceived disloyalty, violations of professional boundaries, and some measure of pathology or character disturbance on the part of either the mentor or mentee. Regardless of the cause, excellent mentors earnestly try to diffuse hostility, correct misunderstandings, and reconcile differences in mentor relationships.

When it becomes apparent that a mentorship cannot be salvaged and that continuation is either impossible or likely to result in additional negative outcomes, either party may terminate the relationship. Although mentors should normally take the lead for ending a mentorship, sometimes a mentee may simply refuse further contact with a mentor. On rare occasions, a mentee may gossip about a former mentor or even file a formal complaint in an effort to exact emotional retribution or sabotage a mentor's career. In these cases, a mentor will be well served to carefully document the development of the conflict. In addition to the mentor's own narrative, careful documentation will include evidence of reflection about the problem, efforts to address the conflict and restore the relationship, any collegial consultation, thoughts about ethical duties and professional requirements, and overarching evidence of concern for the mentee's best interests.

Finally, it is important to note that documentation should be seen as more than just an emergency tool for responding defensively to mentee complaints. Routine documentation of ongoing mentorships is also encouraged as an indicator of intentional and deliberate mentoring excellence. Brief but clear documentation of mentorship formation, early discussions of relationship expectations, and periodic assessments of the mentorship's benefits and outcomes signal to both the mentee and external observers that the mentor is thoughtful and intentional about the mentoring enterprise. Conflict aside, a well-documented mentorship also makes positive mentoring tasks more effective and efficient. Writing letters of recommendation for a previous mentee is a case in point. A small folder of documentation will prove invaluable and allow you to construct a thorough and accurate picture of your mentee.

KEY COMPONENTS

- *Document your mentorships carefully as a way of ensuring good practice and protecting yourself and your mentees from subsequent misrepresentation of the relationship.*

- *Practice terse record-keeping of mentee goals, expectations, achievements, and concerns.*
- *Record instances of conflict or negative interactions as well as clear rationale and description of your response.*
- *Document consultation and efforts to provide corrective feedback and restore the relationship.*

70

Dispute Your Irrational Thinking

As head of a large federal agency, Sandy was a case study in professional and managerial success. In Kathryn, a new managerial trainee and a recent college graduate, Sandy saw a mirror image of herself three decades earlier. Kathryn was smart, interpersonally savvy, and quite ambitious. She worked long hours without complaint. These qualities prompted Sandy to take Kathryn under her wing, beginning what would become a very meaningful mentoring relationship. Things began to change during Kathryn's third year with the agency. Kathryn began dropping hints about taking a couple years off as a "sabbatical" to travel with her spouse, enjoy life a bit, and then reconsider her career opportunities. Although she was happy for Kathryn on one level—even a bit envious at the idea of such a bold life adventure—Sandy found herself reacting to Kathryn with anger, annoyance, and stern warnings about "throwing away a promising career." After one particularly terse conversation, Sandy was startled by the vehemence of her own comments and the intensity of her powerful feelings of disappointment and betrayal. Upon some difficult reflection, Sandy realized she was making several rather extreme evaluations of Kathryn and Kathryn's choices. Some of Sandy's irrational thoughts and demands were, "She should follow my career path and model my example precisely," "She must see that I know best and take my advice," "It is awful and catastrophic that this bright young woman might squander a fine career opportunity!" Not only did Sandy recognize these thoughts and evaluations as extreme, she shared her insights with Kathryn and was able to both laugh at herself and give Kathryn permission to make her own decisions with Sandy's blessing. Ultimately, Kathryn returned to the agency after a year of travel and enjoyed a successful zig-zagging career punctuated by several brief sabbatical years and positions in several different areas of the agency. The mentorship was bolstered by Sandy's insight and willingness to change her "crazy thinking."

When things go wrong in a mentorship, mentors need to know what part they play in the disturbance. They need to ask themselves these questions: "How am *I* making *myself* disturbed?" "What are the flaws in *my* thinking?" "How is *my* disturbance interfering with the relationship?" "How can *I* get beyond the disturbance?"

At times, even the most mature, rational, and seasoned mentor falls prey to pernicious and destructive irrational beliefs. Irrational beliefs are rigid—though often unconscious—demands about self, the mentee, or the relationship. Irrational demands almost always lead to additional irrational thinking such as *harsh evaluations* (e.g., "My mentee is absolutely worthless and should suffer for causing me so much extra work!"), *catastrophic thinking* (e.g., "This is absolutely awful!"), and *poor frustration tolerance* (e.g., "I can't stand this!"). Strong irrational beliefs nearly always lead to emotional upset (e.g., anger, anxiety, depression) and usually make matters with mentees much worse. It may not be surprising that the type of person most likely to become an excellent mentor (e.g., successful, achievement-focused, driven to help others) may be more prone to adopt certain self-defeating irrational tendencies. This type of driven individual sometimes pushes the envelope in his or her thinking patterns.

Examples of irrational beliefs most likely to plague otherwise fine mentors are:

I *must* be successful with all of my mentees all of the time.

I *have to* be greatly respected and loved by all of my mentees.

Because I have invested so much as a mentor, my mentees *should* be equally ambitious and always eager to do exactly what I recommend.

I *must* reap tremendous benefit from mentoring and *should* enjoy mentoring all the time.

My mentees *must* never leave or disappoint me.

Quite often, when mentors are upset and disturbed with either a mentee or with themselves as a mentor, one of these irrational demands bubbles to the top and interferes with resolution and restoration.

In spite of the human proclivity for irrational self-disturbance, excellent mentors adopt several strategies for minimizing the negative impact of irrational thinking. Mentor coping strategies include:

1. acknowledging feeling disturbed or upset while searching for one's contributing irrational demands and evaluations;
2. actively disputing or challenging mentor-related irrational beliefs in front of one's mentees (e.g., "You know, when you neglected to turn in that report as promised, I really got myself enraged at first. Then I realized I was crazily demanding that you be perfect. Now I'm just a

bit annoyed and wondering how I can help you get that report wrapped up");

3. refusing to tell yourself that anything a mentee does (or fails to do) is awful;

4. carefully separating human worth (your own and the mentee's) from performance; and

5. frequently and humorously finding opportunities to display your own fallibility (thus providing a good model of human imperfection for the mentee).

KEY COMPONENTS

- *Recognize your irrational demands of mentees and evaluations of events.*
- *Be alert to signs that you are harshly evaluating, exaggerating, or failing to tolerate frustration.*
- *Actively dispute dysfunctional beliefs about mentees, yourself as mentor, and the ideal mentorship.*
- *Disclose irrational thinking to mentees, laugh at yourself, and show mentees how you correct your own self-defeating thinking.*

· · ·

Welcoming Change and
Saying Goodbye

MATTERS OF CLOSURE

Many mentorships end as anticipated in a planned and timely manner. The mentor and mentee leave the formal part of their relationship on a positive note. On the other hand, too many mentorships end with unfinished business. Some mentors either fail to plan a positive ending or actively avoid the idea of an ending. Their failure reflects a misunderstanding of the necessity of planning, while their avoidance conjures up pain and sadness that sometimes accompany saying goodbye.

In our society, we have a culture of pain avoidance. Because relationship endings can be painful, the intuitive human response is to avoid the discomfort of loss. In his Pulitzer Prize–winning book *The Denial of Death*, Ernest Becker makes the case that human beings phobically and unconsciously avoid basic awareness, let alone active consideration, of the reality of the end of life. Along similar lines, human beings often avoid the reality of the ending of a relationship. This is sometimes true of mentors, even those seasoned and intelligent veterans who have bonded with their mentees. In our experience, too many mentors are poor at managing the final phase of mentoring.

Three primary reasons dominate why mentors fail at this task. First, many people never had graceful endings modeled in their own relationships with mentors. As a result, they do not have a picture of how a healthy ending looks. Second, many people come from family and cultural backgrounds where denial of endings is the norm. When a close friend moves away, people are comfortable saying, "See you around," and then they get back to work. Finally, some mentors simply find it threatening when a mentee leaves. As the mentee pulls away and disengages, mentors may have a host of reactions, including self-protective anger or reactive disengagement. This may bring otherwise good mentorships to pathetic termination.

Mindful mentors understand the importance of preparing for meaningful closure of the mentorship. They come to celebrate mentee transitions and leave-taking. Rather than allowing a long-term mentor relationship to end suddenly or fade away unacknowledged, they make the interior world of thought and emotion—both the mentee's and the mentor's—explicit in a way that brings meaningful closure for both parties. Because of their appreciation of the redefinition phase, they actively arrange opportunities and venues for open discussion of the experience of ending. Great mentors find ways to honor and mark the mentee's increasing autonomy, the decreasing intensity of the mentorship, and the pending end of the mentorship's active phase. A self-aware mentor might express gratitude for the privilege of knowing the mentee, sadness at seeing the mentee move on, and deep satisfaction at the mentee's competence and confidence. When a mentor models open acknowledgment of relational transitions and endings, mentees are blessed. Permission is granted for the mentee to move on. Such experiences are deeply meaningful to mentees and reaffirm the value of the mentorship. Long after the formal mentorship has ended, the mentee should be able to look in retrospect with fondness upon this moment of demarcation.

In this section, we highlight the importance of instilling a mentoring mindset so that your legacy of mentorship continues in new generations, welcoming mentees' development, accepting and embracing the end of relationships, discovering helpful ways to say goodbye, and becoming a mentor as a way of life.

71

Instill a Mentoring Mindset

As one of the rare African American women in the competitive "bro" world of software coding, Jada often smiled to herself, feeling that she'd won the career lottery the day she'd first met her mentor, Richard. A seasoned programmer, project manager, and vice president of the software company, Richard recognized Jada's talent early on and began serving as her mentor. Now, as Richard neared retirement and Jada herself was a rising junior executive in the company, she reflected that she was already quite active as a mentor herself. When she gave it serious thought, Jada realized that much of her own approach to mentoring was patterned after her experience with and observation of Richard over the years. In effect, she had internalized his thoughtful interest, his gracious affirmations, his consistent coaching, and his unfailing collegiality. She smiled at the realization that her mentor had given her a powerful mentoring map.

One of the greatest gifts mentors can give to their mentees is the skill of passing the mentoring baton. In a relay race, each of the four runners in this event take turns running around the track and carrying a baton. Baton-passing starts with the athlete who runs the first leg of the race, continues with the second and third runners, and ends with the anchor carrying the baton across the finish line. A team does not finish the race until each runner completes a full lap around the track while carrying the baton.

The metaphor of baton-passing is useful for describing one of the elements of mentoring—instilling a *mentoring mindset*. What is a mindset? It is a well-established set of attitudes (e.g., "I often notice talented young people in my organization and think of them as rising stars"), beliefs (e.g., "As my own mentor has indicated, I would make a good mentor for others"), and values (e.g., "Caring for the next generation is a worthy and meaningful enterprise"). According to renowned Stanford University psychologist Carol Dweck, a mindset actually is a simple but powerful concept. She says that it makes all the difference in the world of how people behave and make decisions. By consciously and conscientiously instilling a mentoring mindset in their own mentees, mentors exponentially increase their impact by cultivating a generation of new mentors.

Look at the power of instilling a mentoring mindset, along with the difference it can make in the world. Any mentor who effectively develops a mentee makes an incredible contribution to the mentee, who then contributes incredibly to the organization and the larger society. The contribution derives from the mentee's self-efficacy, skills, and talents, which were honed through mentoring. However, mentors can go a step further. They can instill in that same mentee a set of attitudes, beliefs, and values that reflect a commitment to mentoring other mentees to become mentors. This achievement can lead to an immeasurable contribution: a legacy of mentoring.

Let us revisit the metaphor of baton-passing in a relay. Instilling a mentoring mindset can be more impactful than passing a single baton. For one thing, each runner passes the same baton to only one other runner. In mentoring, a mentor can pass the baton to many mentees, not just to one. For another, mentors can instill in each of their mentees a mindset of then imparting the mentoring mindset to their own mentees. Ultimately, mentoring with the aim of instilling a mentoring mindset has no finish line. The activity can be endless. This element reminds us of the difference between addition and multiplication—mentoring one mentee at a time or mentoring for exponential mentoring. Any mentor, as we can see, has the potential of making maximal impact if they multiply mentees.

Instilling a mentoring mindset is much like creating a schema or a mental map for how good mentoring works. Think of it as a mentoring relationship blueprint. It translates the essential attitudes, beliefs, and values of the mindset into actionable behaviors. Of course, your own role-modeling as a reliable and exemplary mentor is the most important ingredient in creating a mentoring blueprint for your mentees. Years from now, they will call up your example over and over again as they step into the mentor role themselves. Of course, the elements in this book can help you become the exemplary mentor you need to be to pass on quality mentoring traits.

The mentoring relationship between your authors illustrates the multiplication principle and passing of the mentoring baton: Chuck was Brad's mentor in graduate school. Brad subsequently began to do research and writing on mentoring. More important, Brad began to mentor a generation of young scholars, many of whom have gone on to become prolific mentors themselves, and some have even conducted research on mentoring relationships. This monumental impact is something Chuck could never have imagined when he first began mentoring Brad more than thirty years ago.

KEY COMPONENTS

- *Amplify the impact of your mentoring work by deliberately instilling a mentoring mindset in your mentees.*
- *Deliberately work to nurture in your own mentees the*

attitudes, beliefs, and values consistent with intentional mentoring.

- *Remember that your own example (attitudes and behaviors) will become a powerful schema or mentoring map for your mentees moving forward.*

72

Welcome Change and Growth

When Bob transferred to the company's marketing division, Gale liked him immediately. A senior marketing team manager, Gale was delighted to have a bright and energetic trainee with whom to share his experience and marketing savvy. Inquisitive by nature and eager to watch Gale at work, Bob proved to be a quick study, and he soon was making valuable contributions to the creative team's brainstorming sessions and marketing research. Within the year, Gale was including Bob in all of the company's marketing projects, and their relationship flourished. During Bob's third year with the team, Gale realized that Bob needed less career advice and very little direct supervision. Bob actually began to outpace Gale. He became more productive and creative. Initially, Gale was threatened and disheartened. In Gale's mind, mentors are supposed to outpace mentees. Eventually, Gale realized Bob's success was at least partially related to their good mentorship. With this realization, Gale began commenting on Bob's professional growth and the changing nature of their connection—from mentorship to collegial friendship. These efforts heightened Bob's confidence as well as his appreciation for Gale's support.

All relationships evolve and change. If the changes are not fruitful, stagnation or deterioration set in, signaling that something is drastically wrong in the mentorship. By their nature, mentorships are developmental relationships, focused on the transition of the mentee from neophyte to full member of a profession. Mentors should remember, though, that mentorships grow at different rates—each according to a number of factors. Expectations vary. Although change is a requisite of healthy mentoring, there is tremendous variation in the rate or trajectory of change. Some mentees race to test their skills as independent professionals, while others are timid and reluctant. Some mentors are better facilitators of change than others. Additionally, mentees begin at different places on the trajectory of change. Some are simply more advanced, knowledgeable, or experienced than others. Although growth and change are the very essence of mentoring, some pain and adjustment inevitably accompany mentorship transitions.

One time when pain is particularly noticeable is when the mentee—in a close and long-term mentorship—begins the process of separating from the mentor. Both parties may experience turmoil, anxiety, loss, and general disruption. Either party may consciously or unconsciously resist the change—clinging to the way things used to be. For example, in an effort to preserve a valued relationship, a mentor may ignore the fundamental ethical requirement to promote mentee autonomy and independence, opting instead to foster dependency and withhold endorsement of the mentee's competence.

Management professor Kathy Kram identified four common phases of mentorship development. Excellent mentors should become familiar with these phases, understand the unique needs of mentees in each phase, and acknowledge and welcome transition to a new phase. The first phase of mentorship development, *initiation*, is marked by excitement, possibility, and beginning. The mentee often feels anxious, overwhelmed, and dependent on the mentor. New mentees may feel unqualified and inadequate professionally—an imposter waiting to be revealed. Although mentees usually are open to feedback, coachable, and enjoyable to work with during this phase, mentors must be cautious not to encourage mentees to clone themselves in the image of the mentor.

Phase two, *cultivation*, typically begins after several months and is often the most productive phase of the mentorship. During this period, which often lasts at least a year or two, mentees demonstrate increasing competence and confidence. They begin to establish a professional identity—often assimilating their mentor's example into their own personal style. During this phase, it is essential for the mentor to entrust the mentee with increasing responsibility and autonomy. Mentors must also allow the relationship to become more reciprocal and collegial.

In the third phase, *separation*, the mentorship is characterized by leave-taking and distancing. This may be a difficult time emotionally, as both parties must accept some loss and arrange to say goodbye to the intensive phase of the relationship. As the mentorship becomes (quite appropriately) less central in the life of the mentee, a mentor may experience loss, anger, or even insecurity at the mentee's new competence. Excellent mentors work through these feelings, intentionally endorse the mentee's status as colleague, and reinforce the mentee's sense of autonomy. Emotionally mature mentors delight in the competence and high achievements of their mentees, even when their achievements surpass those of the mentor.

Whatever the phase of mentorship development or the rate of mentee growth, the important thing is for the mentor to welcome change. It is helpful for the mentor to take the lead in occasionally discussing the status of the mentorship. Important questions to ask include the following: How far has the mentee come? Where is he or she going? Are there noticeable changes in the nature of the relationship, the mentee's competence, and the mentor's view of the mentee as professional? Good mentors celebrate growth and change with their mentees even when change brings about loss. They understand that celebration is a memorable marker of transition.

KEY COMPONENTS

- *Accept the fact that good mentoring will ensure growth in your mentee and change in your relationship.*
- *Recognize that development and independence in mentees requires you to tolerate some sadness and make adjustments.*
- *Understand the common phases of mentorship development and how your mentee might need different things from you at each phase.*
- *Narrate, welcome, and even highlight evidence of mentee independence.*

73

Accept Endings

Myrna was sometimes humorously referred to as the "czar" of the university's chemistry department. As the department chair and faculty leader for nearly two decades, Myrna was a trove of wisdom and a force to be reckoned with when it came to policy and decision-making. Myrna was particularly fond of mentoring some of her most promising young faculty. Over the years, she had become acquainted with the common seasons of mentorships and had learned, sometimes painfully, to anticipate and even welcome significant changes and transitions in the lives of these treasured relationships. Although Myrna had been most troubled by the separation phase of mentorships with students and faculty early in her career, she had learned— the hard way in some instances—that reluctance to let a mentee mature and become independent was a surefire way to stifle growth or place mentees in a painful double bind (either remain dependent and highly connected or break away from the mentor entirely). As a result, Myrna had become proactive in anticipating and openly acknowledging the separation and redefinition seasons of mentorships. She acknowledged the mixed experience of sadness and satisfaction at seeing skilled faculty move on in their careers, and she found creative and meaningful rituals for marking these transitions.

The final phase of mentorship development, as described by Kathy Kram, is called the *redefinition* phase. After the separation phase, mentor and mentee may continue a collegial friendship characterized by less frequent and informal contact. As the mentee achieves peer status with the mentor, he or she often feels gratitude and appreciation for the mentor's guidance while the mentor continues to support the mentee's career and take pride in the mentee's accomplishments. Mature mentors are delighted even when a mentee's achievements surpass their own achievements.

This ideal outcome requires both mentor and mentee to work through any strong feeling associated with ending the working phase of the mentorship. Outstanding mentors help mentees articulate and work through feelings of sadness or anxiety associated with letting go. Simultaneously, they acknowledge and manage their own sadness, anger, or anxiety at the prospect of losing such an important and close professional connection. In the worst cases, both mentor and mentee may collude to avoid the subject of termination altogether, attempting to go on as if no change has occurred and as if the mentee will require the mentor's intense oversight and attention forever. But such collusion only serves to stunt the mentee's growth and ultimately reduce the value of the mentorship.

Healthy mentors appreciate the seasons of a mentoring relationship. They anticipate and gracefully embrace relationship transitions and take the lead in discussing these with their mentees. Healthy mentors accept endings when mentorships have run their course and facilitate closure when it is time for a mentee to move on and function independently. Excellent mentors help their mentees to appreciate the past but also welcome the future. They help mentees see that the end of the active phase of a mentorship signals success and that any other outcome would be cause for concern.

KEY COMPONENTS

- *Work hard at recognizing and accepting mentorship transitions and endings.*
- *Allow yourself to accept and experience sadness and loss when a particularly close mentorship becomes less active and requires redefinition.*
- *Model acceptance of ending for mentees and initiate explicit discussions about how each party experiences relationship changes.*
- *Reframe change and even endings as inevitable and indicative of mentorship success.*

74

Find Helpful Ways to Say Goodbye

After five years of mentoring Adrian, Sam had come to see her as part managerial superstar in the making, part creative colleague, and part beloved "daughter." Sam had recognized Adrian's unusual leadership talent during her first year with the company and had chosen her from a vast pool of junior managers to become the assistant vice president of human relations. In this role, Adrian had flourished—at least partly as a result of Sam's strong advocacy, coaching, challenge, and encouragement. Adrian's work had begun to attract the attention of other vice presidents and the board of directors. She soon was offered a major promotion and a vice presidency of a division. Though surprised by his own ambivalence at her success (delighted for her success yet honestly saddened by her departure), Sam recognized both the importance of this promotion for Adrian's career and the difficulty she was having sharing her decision to move on with him. To give her permission to move on, and simultaneously to recognize an important transition in the mentorship, Sam scheduled a lunch meeting with Adrian. During the meeting, he offered a retrospective of their mentorship, starting with his early perceptions of her unique talents, his delight in their synergistic and creative working relationship, and his pleasure and pride in her remarkable accomplishments. He emphasized the ways in which the mentorship had been helpful to him professionally and meaningful personally. Sam also acknowledged the ending of the active phase of their mentorship and described his mixture of sadness and gratitude at coming to this transition. This parting ritual proved profoundly meaningful to Adrian who was freed to express her own ambivalence about leaving and her deep ap-

preciation for Sam's graceful support. Their contact grew less
frequent, but they continued to support each other for years.

Preparing to say goodbye to a mentee is among the most over-looked yet richly satisfying elements of successful mentoring. Quite often, only the most seasoned mentors carefully honor endings. Excellent mentors find creative methods for recognizing and honoring good collaboration, strong friendship, and important professional growth in a mentee. Such recognition is particularly important at salient transition points between phases in a mentorship or when a mentorship has run its course and is moving toward long-term ending or redefinition. Saying goodbye requires self-awareness and the ability to both experience and articulate feelings about the mentee and about allowing the mentee to move on.

One of the most effective methods of bringing closure to a mentorship is to schedule a formal time to process and celebrate the mentee's moving on. This may take the form of a lunch or dinner meeting or just a conversation over a cup of coffee. A formal meeting offers the mentor an opportunity to say goodbye to the mentee through the medium of storytelling; the mentor offers a narrative of the mentorship, including salient highlights of the mentee's developmental milestones and things about the mentee that have most impressed the mentor. By weaving the history of the mentorship into a coherent narrative, mentors allow mentees to clearly reflect on their growth and accomplishments through the lens of the mentor.

Mentors also may helpfully disclose their own feelings about the mentorship, the mentee, and about the pending transition or ending. By giving voice to important emotions and experiences, mentors free their mentees to do the same. In many cases, a mentee will avoid formally saying goodbye to a mentor unless the mentor takes the lead—offering a model of how to do this well.

As mentor and mentee share reflections and express gratitude for one another, relationship closure occurs. Both parties are free to take leave, redefine the relationship, and move forward with new endeavors and perhaps different mentorships.

KEY COMPONENTS

- *Say goodbye to your mentee and explicitly acknowledge the end of a mentorship.*
- *Arrange a specific meeting or interaction for the purpose of saying goodbye and formally recognizing change in the relationship.*
- *Provide your mentee with a personal narrative of the mentorship, including your own sense of gratitude about knowing the mentee.*
- *Be sure to acknowledge intangible gifts received and lessons learned from the mentee.*

75
Mentor as a Way of Life

Although he had been retired from the school district for nearly ten years, Henry continued to serve as coach, confidant, encourager, and sponsor to several generations of high school students, teachers, and administrators. During a 40-year career in education, Henry had gone from first-year science teacher to becoming the first African American principal of the largest high school in the state. Naturally inclined to helping juniors, Henry was beloved by several generations of African American men and women whom he mentored in the teaching profession. Many had become successful administrators, emulating their mentor. Known for his open-door policy, keen interpersonal skills, and genuine interest in the lives of his students and teachers, Henry had profoundly touched the lives of hundreds of mentees. Although happy to give up his administrative duties at retirement, Henry continued to savor relationships with younger teachers and the opportunity to share his wisdom and propel their careers through letters of recommendation, sponsorship, and support. Although Henry's wife sometimes expressed good-natured exasperation at his continued involvement in the lives of his many mentees, he derived great satisfaction from developing talent in others. Henry remained a powerful and influential mentor to young educators until his death.

Authentic mentors—those for whom the commitment is personal as well as professional—never stop mentoring. Throughout their careers, mentoring becomes a deeply engrained and consistently expressed facet of the mentor's personhood. Seldom do master mentors' inclinations toward helping lie dormant or untapped. For many of them, their inclinations do not cease and desist even in retirement. Somehow they find ways to invest, at least informally, in the development of others. As the title of this element aptly states, mentoring is "a way of life."

Research indicates that excellent mentors manifest a general personality tendency or interest in caring for younger and less experienced individuals. This is often referred to as *generative concern*. While the full potential of this quality may be harnessed, generative concern cannot be taught or trained. It either exists in the fundamental core of the mentor's personality or it does not. Mentors who are generative and caring by nature are those who endure in the mentor role. Not surprisingly, generativity is strongly related to openness, emotional stability, and agreeableness. These mentors often help scores of mentees during their lifetime and many of their mentorships continue as strong collegial friendships for years.

Mentoring becomes a way of life for outstanding mentors for two basic reasons. They delight in seeing their mentees succeed. On this point, they know what the success means to the mentees, and they know the potential contributions to be realized through their success. They also reap rich internal rewards; they know that few things compare in personal fulfillment as the positive outcomes of their investments in mentees. Research on generative men and women show that they report greater levels of happiness and general life satisfaction than people who are not generative. The tendency for these generative souls to mentor is so automatic that not mentoring is never a viable consideration for them. Although mentors choose mentees selectively and safeguard their own time and resources so that they are productive, helpful for mentees, and attentive to their personal self-care, generative mentors are persistently drawn to mentoring others.

We conclude this chapter and book with a final word of sage advice. You cannot mentor everyone. Thus, to successfully mentor across an entire career, revisit our very first element: set limits and be selective.

KEY COMPONENTS

- *Make mentoring a common component of your ongoing life and work.*
- *Remember that if you are drawn to mentoring, you probably have gifts in this area that will be best served by frequent use.*
- *Recognize the rich rewards associated with mentoring, but take care to protect yourself from becoming overextended.*

Appendix

A MENTORING CODE OF ETHICS

Adhering to general moral and ethical principles is an important first step in living out an ethical commitment to mentees. The following *Mentoring Code of Ethics* contains eight ethical principles for the practice of mentoring. These principles serve as the foundation for ethical mentor behavior and decision-making.

- *Beneficence: Mentors strive to facilitate the growth and contribute to the welfare of their mentees. Mentors are obligated to promote mentees' best interests and to consider the unique developmental needs of each mentee.*
- *Nonmaleficence: Mentors work to avoid intentional or unintended harm to those they mentor. Mentors endeavor to avoid neglect, abandonment, or exploitation of mentees and are cautious to prevent boundary violations.*
- *Autonomy: Mentors endeavor to strengthen mentees' knowledge, maturity, and independence. They work against both intellectual and relational dependency in their mentorships and instead promote a mentee's creativity, independence, and sense of self in the profession.*

- *Justice:* Mentors ensure fair and equitable treatment of mentees regardless of variables such as race, ethnicity, gender, sexual orientation, and age. Mentors try to ensure equal access by prospective mentees representing the full range of diversity present in the organization or educational program.

- *Transparency:* Mentors are open and transparent about all of their mentorships; they avoid even the appearance of hiding the nature of a relationship with a mentee and they encourage open communication with mentees about mutual expectations in the relationship.

- *Boundaries and Multiple Relationships:* Mentors are careful to honor boundaries in their relationships with mentees and cautious about entering any new relationship with a mentee that could compromise the value of the mentorship or harm the mentee.

- *Privacy:* Mentors protect information shared with them in confidence by mentees. If a disclosure is necessary, for example, to keep a mentee safe or prevent harm to others, the mentor attempts to discuss this exception to privacy with the mentee in advance of the disclosure.

- *Competence:* Mentors consistently work at establishing, developing, and sharpening their skill set and mindset in the mentor role.

References

Allen, T. D. (2003). Mentoring others: A dispositional and motivational approach. *Journal of Vocational Behavior* 62, 134–154.

Allen, T. D., & Eby, L. T. (2004). Factors related to mentor reports of mentoring functions provided: Gender and relational characteristics. *Sex Roles* 50, 129–139.

Allen, T. D., & Eby, L. T. (2007). *Blackwell handbook of mentoring: A multiple perspectives approach.* London: Blackwell.

Allen, T. D., Eby, L. T., & Lentz, E. (2006). The relationship between formal mentoring program characteristics and perceived program effectiveness. *Personnel Psychology* 59, 125–153.

Allen, T. D., Finkelstein, L. M., & Poteet, M. L. (2009). *Designing workplace mentoring programs.* New York: Wiley-Blackwell.

Allen, T. D., & Poteet, M. L. (1999). Developing effective mentoring relationships: Strategies from the mentor's viewpoint. *The Career Development Quarterly* 48, 59–73.

Allen, T. D., Poteet, M. L., & Burroughs, S. M. (1997). The mentor's perspective: A qualitative inquiry and future research agenda. *Journal of Vocational Behavior* 51, 70–89.

Allen, T. D., Poteet, M. L., & Russell, J. E. A. (2000). Protégé selection by mentors: What makes the difference? *Journal of Organizational Behavior* 21, 271–282.

Barnett, J. E. (2008). Mentoring, boundaries, and multiple relationships: Opportunities and challenges. *Mentoring and Tutoring: Partnership in Learning* 16, 3–16.

Barnett, S. K. (1984). The mentor role: A task of generativity. *Journal of Human Behavior and Learning* 1, 15–18.

Billimoria, D., Joy, S., & Liang, X. (2008). Breaking barriers and creating inclusiveness: Lessons of organizational transformation to advance women faculty in academic science and engineering. *Human Resources Management* 47, 423–441.

Blackburn, R. T., Chapman, D. W., & Cameron, S. M. (1981). "Cloning" in academia: Mentorship and academic careers. *Research in Higher Education* 15, 315–327.

Boice, R. (1992). *The new faculty member: Supporting and fostering professional development*. San Francisco: Jossey-Bass.

Bornstein, R. F. (1989). Exposure and affect: Overview and meta-analysis of research, 1968–1987. *Psychological Bulletin* 106, 265–289.

Bowlby, J. (1969). *Attachment and loss: Vol 1: Attachment*. New York: Basic Books.

Brown, K. T., & Ostrove, J. M. (2013). What does it mean to be an ally? The perception of allies from the perspective of people of color. *Journal of Applied Social Psychology* 43, 2211–2222.

Burke, R. J. (1984). Mentors in organizations. *Group and Organizational Studies* 9, 353–372.

Chao, G. T. (1997). Mentoring phases and outcomes. *Journal of Vocational Behavior* 51, 15–28.

Chao, G. T. (2009). Formal mentoring: Lessons learned from past practice. *Professional Psychology: Research and Practice* 40, 314–320.

Chao, G. T., Walz, P. M., & Gardner, P. D. (1992). Formal and informal mentorships: A comparison on mentoring functions and contrast with nonmentored counterparts. *Personnel Psychology* 45, 619–636.

Cherniss, C. (2007). The role of emotional intelligence in the mentoring process. In B. R. Ragins & K. E. Kram (eds.), *The handbook of mentoring at work: Theory, research, and practice* (pp. 427–446). Los Angeles: Sage.

Clutterbuck, D. A., Kochan, F., Lunsford, L. G., Dominguez, N., & Haddock-Millar, J. (2017). *The SAGE handbook of mentoring*. Thousand Oaks, CA: Sage.

Crosby, F. J. (1999). The developing literature on developmental relationships. In A. J. Murrell, F. J. Crosby, & R. J. Ely (eds.), *Mentoring dilemmas: Developmental relationships within multicultural organizations* (pp. 3–20). Mahwah, NJ: Lawrence Erlbaum.

Davis, L. L., Little, M. S., & Thornton, W. L. (1997). The art and angst of the mentoring relationship. *Academic Psychiatry* 21, 61–71.

DeLong, T. J., Gabarro, J. J., & Lees, R. J. (January 2008). Why mentoring matters in a hypercompetitive world. *Harvard Business Review* 86, 115–121.

Donaldson, S. I., Ensher, E. A., & Grant-Vallone, E. J. (2000). Longitudinal examination of mentoring relationships on organizational commitment and citizenship behavior. *Journal of Career Development* 26, 233–249.

Dreher, G. F., & Ash, R. A. (1990). A comparative study of mentoring among men and women in managerial, professional, and technical positions. *Journal of Applied Psychology* 75, 539–546.

Drigotas, S., Rusbult, C., Wieselquist, J., & Whitton, S. (1999). Close partner as sculptor of the ideal self: Behavioral affirmation and the Michelangelo Phenomenon. *Journal of Personality and Social Psychology* 77, 293–323.

DuBois, D. L., Portillo, N., Rhodes, J. E., Silverthorn, N., & Valentine, J. C. (2011). How effective are mentoring programs for youth? A systematic assessment of the evidence. *Psychological Sciences in the Public Interest* 12, 57–91.

Duck, S. (1994). Stratagems, spoils, and a serpent's tooth: On the delights and dilemmas of personal relationships. In W. R. Cupach & B. H. Spitzberg (eds.), *The dark side of interpersonal communication* (pp. 3–24). Hillsdale, NJ: Lawrence Erlbaum.

Dweck, C. (2007/2016). *Mindset: The new psychology of success.* New York: Ballantine Books.

Eby, L. T., & Allen, T. D. (2002). Further investigation of protégés' negative mentoring experiences: Patterns and outcomes. *Group and Organization Management* 27, 456–479.

Eby, L. T., Allen, T. D., Evans, S. C., Ng, T., & DuBois, D. L. (2008). Does mentoring matter? A multidisciplinary meta-analysis comparing mentored and non-mentored individuals. *Journal of Vocational Behavior* 72, 254–267.

Eby, L. T., Lockwood, A. L., & Butts, M. (2006). Perceived support for mentoring: A multiple perspectives approach. *Journal of Vocational Behavior* 68, 267–291.

Elliott, C. J., Leck, J. D., Orser, B., & Mossop, C. (2011). An exploration of gender and trust in mentoring relationships. *Journal of Diversity Management* 1, 1–12.

Ensher, E. A., & Murphy, S. E. (1997). Effects of race, gender, perceived similarity, and contact on mentor relationships. *Journal of Vocational Behavior* 50, 460–481.

Ensher, E. A., & Murphy, S. E. (2011). The mentoring relationship challenges scale: The impact of mentoring stage, type, and gender. *Journal of Vocational Behavior* 79, 253–266.

Erikson, E. H. (1959/1980). *Identity and the life cycle.* New York: Norton.

Fagenson-Eland, E. A., Marks, M. A., & Amendola, K. L. (1997). Perceptions of mentoring relationships. *Journal of Vocational Behavior* 51, 29–42.

Felton, P., Bauman, H-D. L., Kheriaty, A., & Taylor, E. (2013). *Transformative conversations: A guide to mentoring communities among colleagues in higher education.* San Francisco: Jossey-Bass.

Flum, H. (2001). Relational dimensions in career development. *Journal of Vocational Behavior* 59, 1–16.

Forehand, R. L. (2008). The art and science of mentoring in psychology: A necessary practice to ensure our future. *American Psychologist* 63, 744–755.

Gentry, W. A., & Sosik, J. J. (2010). Developmental relationships and managerial promotability in organizations: A multisource study. *Journal of Vocational Behavior* 77, 266–278.

Ghosh, R., & Reio, T. G. (2013). Career benefits associated with mentoring for mentors: A meta-analysis. *Journal of Vocational Behavior* 83, 106–116.

Goleman, D. (1995). *Emotional intelligence.* New York: Bantam Books.

Griffin, K. A., & Reddick, R. J. (2011). Surveillance and sacrifice: Gender differences in the mentoring patterns of black professors at predominantly white research universities. *American Educational Research Journal* 48, 1032–1057.

Gunn, J. E., & Pistole, M. C. (2012). Trainee supervisor attachment: Explaining the alliance and disclosure in supervision. *Training and Education in Professional Psychology* 6, 229–337.

Haggard, D. L., Dougherty, T. W., Turban, D. B., & Wilbanks, J. E. (2011). Who is a mentor? A review of evolving definitions and implications for research. *Journal of Management* 37, 280–304.

Haggard, D. L., & Turban, D. B. (2012). The mentoring relationship as a context for psychological contract development. *Journal of Applied Social Psychology* 42, 1904–1931.

Hewlett, S. A., Peraino, K., Sherbin, L., & Sumberg, K. (2010). *The sponsor effect: Breaking through the last glass ceiling.* Cambridge, MA: Harvard Business Review.

Higgins, M. C., Chandler, D. E., & Kram, K. E. (2007). Developmental initiation and developmental networks. In B. R. Ragins & K. E. Kram (eds.), *The handbook of mentoring at work: Theory, research, and practice* (pp. 349–372). Thousand Oaks, CA: Sage.

Higgins, M. C., & Kram, K. E. (2001). Reconceptualizing mentoring at work: A developmental network perspective. *Academy of Management Review* 26, 264–288.

Higgins, M. C., & Thomas, D. A. (2001). Constellations and careers: Toward understanding the effects of multiple developmental relationships. *Journal of Organizational Behavior* 22, 223–247.

Hill, C. E., & O'Brien, K. M. (2014). *Helping skills: Facilitating exploration, insight, and action* (4th ed.). Washington, DC: American Psychological Association.

Hook, J. N., Davis, D. E., Owen, J., Worthington, E. L., & Utsey, S. O. (2013). Cultural humility: Measuring openness to culturally diverse clients. *Journal of Counseling Psychology* 60, 353–366.

Jacobi, M. (1991). Mentoring and undergraduate academic success: A literature review. *Review of Educational Research* 64, 505–532.

Johnson, W. B. (2002). The intentional mentor: Strategies and guidelines for the practice of mentoring. *Professional Psychology: Research and Practice* 33, 88–96.

Johnson, W. B. (2003). A framework for conceptualizing competence to mentor. *Ethics & Behavior* 13, 127–151.

Johnson, W. B. (2015). *On being a mentor: A guide for higher education faculty* (2nd ed.). New York: Routledge.

Johnson, W. B., & Huwe, J. M. (2003). *Getting mentored in graduate school.* Washington, DC: American Psychological Association.

Johnson, W. B., Huwe, J. M., & Lucas, J. L. (2000). Rational mentoring. *Journal of Rational-Emotive and Cognitive-Behavior Therapy* 18, 39–54.

Johnson, W. B., & Ridley, C. R. (2008). *The elements of ethics.* New York: Palgrave Macmillan.

Johnson, W. B., Skinner, C. J., & Kaslow, N. J. (2014). Relational mentoring in clinical supervision: The transformational supervisor. *Journal of Clinical Psychology: In Session* 70, 1073–1081.

Johnson, W. B., & Smith, D. (2016). *Athena rising: How and why men should mentor women.* New York: Routledge.

Johnson-Bailey, J., & Cervero, R. M. (2004). Mentoring in black and white: The intricacies of cross-cultural mentoring. *Mentoring and Tutoring* 12, 7–21.

Kendi, I. (2016). *Stamped from the beginning: The definitive history of racist ideas in America.* New York: Nation Books.

King, M. L. (August 1963). Letter from Birmingham Jail, published as "The Negro Is Your Brother" in *The Atlantic Monthly* 212(2), 78–88.

Kluckholn, C., & Murray, H. A. (1953). *Personality in nature, society, and culture* (2nd ed.). New York: Knopf.

Kram, K. E. (1983). Phases of the mentor relationship. *Academy of Management Journal* 26, 608–625.

Kram, K. E. (1985). *Mentoring at work: Developmental relationships in organizational life.* Glenview, IL: Scott Foresman.

Lee, A., Dennis, C., & Campbell, P. (2007). Nature's guide for mentors. *Nature* 447, 791–797.

Levinson, D. J., Darrow, C. N., Klein, E. B., Levinson, M. H., & McKee, B. (1978). *The seasons of a man's life.* New York: Ballantine.

Loden, M. (May 2011). On feminine leadership. *Pelican Bay Post.*

Lunsford, L. G. (2016). *A handbook for managing mentoring programs: Starting, supporting, and sustaining.* New York: Routledge.

Markus, H., & Nurius, P. (1986). Possible selves. *American Psychologist* 41, 954–969.

Marwit, S. J., & Burke, R. J. (2000). Role of deceased mentors in the ongoing lives of protégés. *Journal of Death and Dying* 41, 125–138.

Moberg, D. J., & Velasquez, M. (2004). The ethics of mentoring. *Business Ethics Quarterly* 14, 95–122.

Mullen, C. A. (2004). *Mentorship primer.* New York: Peter Lang.

Nakamura, J., & Shernoff, D. J. (2009). *Good mentoring: Fostering excellent practice in higher education.* New York: Wiley.

Noe, R. A. (1988). An investigation of the determinants of successful assigned mentoring relationships. *Personnel Psychology* 41, 457–479.

Noe, R. A. (1988). Women and mentoring: A review and research agenda. *Academy of Management Review* 13, 65–78.

Noe, R. A., Greenberger, D. B., & Wang, S. (2003). Mentoring: What we know and where we might go. *Research in Personnel and Human Resources Management* 21, 129–173.

O'Brien, K. E., Biga, A., Kessler, S. R., & Allen, T. D. (2010). A meta-analytic investigation of gender differences in mentoring. *Journal of Management* 36, 537–554.

Oglensky, B. D. (2008). The ambivalent dynamics of loyalty in mentorship. *Human Relations* 61, 419–448.

Olian, J. D., Carroll, S. J., & Giannantonio, C. M. (1993). Mentor reactions to protégés: An experiment with managers. *Journal of Vocational Behavior* 43, 266–278.

Peluchette, J. V. E., & Jeanquart, S. (2000). Professionals' use of different mentor sources at various career stages: Implications for career success. *Journal of Social Psychology* 140, 549–564.

Pfund, C., Pribbenow, D. M., Branchaw, J., Lauffer, S. M., & Handelsman, J. (2006). The merits of training mentors. *Science* 311 (5760), 473–474.

Raabe, B., & Beehr, T. A. (2003). Formal mentoring versus supervisor and coworker relationships: Differences in perceptions and impact. *Journal of Organizational Behavior* 24, 271–293.

Ragins, B. R. (2007). Diversity and workplace mentoring relationships: A review and positive social capital approach. In T. D. Allen & L. T. Eby (eds.), *The Blackwell handbook of mentoring: A multiple perspectives approach* (pp. 281–300). Malden, MA: Blackwell.

Ragins, B. R. (2012). Relational mentoring: A positive approach to mentoring at work. In K. S. Cameron & G. M. Spreitzer (eds.), *The Oxford handbook of positive organizational scholarship* (pp. 519–536). New York: Oxford University Press.

Ragins, B. R., & Cotton, J. L. (1999). Mentor functions and outcomes: A comparison of men and women in formal and informal mentoring relationships. *Journal of Applied Psychology* 84, 529–550.

Ragins, B. R., & Kram, K. E. (2007). The roots and meaning of mentoring. In B. R. Ragins & K. E. Kram. *The handbook of mentoring at work: Theory, research and practice* (pp. 3–15). Los Angeles: Sage.

Ramanan, R. A., Phillips, R. S., Davis, R. B., Silen, W., Reede, J. Y. (2002). Mentoring in medicine: Keys to satisfaction. *American Journal of Medicine* 112, 336–341.

Ramaswami, A., Dreher, G. F., Bretz, R., & Wiethoff, C. (2010). Gender, mentoring, and career success: The importance of organizational context. *Personnel Psychology* 63, 385–405.

Ridley, C. R. (2005). *Overcoming unintentional racism in counseling and therapy: A practitioner's guide to intentional intervention* (2nd ed.). Thousand Oaks, CA: Sage.

Roche, G. R. (1979). Much ado about mentors. *Harvard Business Review* 57, 14–28.

Rogers, C. R. (1961). *On becoming a person.* Boston: Houghton Mifflin.

Rusbult, C. E., Finkel, E. J., & Kumashiro, M. (2009). The Michelangelo Phenomenon. *Current Directions in Psychological Science* 18, 305–309.

Russell, G. M., & Horne, S. G. (2009). Finding equilibrium: Mentoring, sexual orientation, and gender-identity. *Professional Psychology: Research and Practice* 40, 194–200.

Seligman, M. E. P., & Maier, S. F. (1967). Failure to escape traumatic shock. *Journal of Experimental Psychology* 74, 1–9.

Sternberg, R. J. (1995). Love as a story. *Journal of Social and Personal Relationships* 12, 541–546.

Strunk, W., & White, E. B. (2000). *The elements of style.* Boston: Allyn & Bacon.

Sue, D. W., & Sue, D. (2012). *Counseling the culturally diverse: Theory and practice* (6th ed.). New York: Wiley.

Swap, W., Leonard, D., Shields, M., & Abrams, L. (2001). Using mentoring and storytelling to transfer knowledge in the workplace. *Journal of Management Information Systems* 18, 95–114.

Thomas, D. A. (2001). Race matters: The truth about mentoring minorities. *Harvard Business Review* 79, 99–107.

Turban, D. B., & Dougherty, T. W. (1994). Role of protégé personality in receipt of mentoring and career success. *Academy of Management Journal* 37, 688–702.

Underhill, C. M. (2005). The effectiveness of mentoring programs in corporate settings: A meta-analytical review of the literature. *Journal of Vocational Behavior* 68, 292–307.

Wanberg, C. R., Kammeyer-Mueller, J., & Marchese, M. (2006). Mentor and protégé predictors and outcomes of mentoring in a formal mentoring program. *Journal of Vocational Behavior* 69, 410–423.

Wang, S., Tomlinson, E. C., & Noe, R. A. (2010). The role of mentor trust and protégé internal locus of control in formal mentoring relationships. *Journal of Applied Psychology* 95, 358–367.

Weil, V. (2001). Mentoring: Some ethical considerations. *Science and Engineering Ethics* 7, 471–482.

Williams, J. C., & Dempsey, R. (2014). *What works for women at work.* New York: New York University Press.

Wilson, P. F., & Johnson, W. B. (2001). Core virtues for the practice of mentoring. *Journal of Psychology and Theology* 29, 121–130.

Zachary, L. J. (2005). *Creating a mentoring culture: The organization's guide.* San Francisco: Jossey-Bass.

Zey, M. G. (1991). *The mentor connection: Strategic alliances in corporate life.* New Brunswick, NJ: Transaction.

Zuckerman, H. (1977). *Scientific elite: Nobel laureates in the United States.* New York: Free Press.

Index